DATED MATERIAL

Tne law and the forms change now and then
which is why this book is printed 2 or 3 times each year.
Make sure you are using the latest printing.
DO NOT USE AN OLD EDITION OF THIS BOOK.
Please call your local bookstore
to make sure you have the latest printing.

THIS BOOK WAS PRINTED IN
JANUARY, 1983

Printing History

June 1971	February 1977
January 1972	June
May	November
November	December
March 1973	June 1978
August	January 1979
November	August
May 1974	January 1980
August	March
December	August
May 1975	February 1981
September	August
November	January 1982
April 1976	May
August	January 1983

ISBN 0-917316-42-8

HOW TO DO YOUR OWN
DIVORCE
IN CALIFORNIA
TENTH EDITION

By California Attorney
CHARLES E. SHERMAN

NOLO PRESS

P.O. Box 544, Occidental, CA 95465

Table of Contents

Part One
All About Divorce

Part Two
How To Do Your Own Regular Dissolution

Part Three
How To Do Your Own Summary Dissolution

READ ALL ABOUT IT!

• NOLO UPDATE SERVICE •

The laws, forms and procedures can change from time to time, and in such a way as might affect your case. It doesn't happen very often, but why take chances? Mail us the coupon below, together with a <u>stamped</u>, <u>self-addressed</u> <u>envelope</u>, and we will notify you of any changes which have occurred, or which may occur in the following six months.

HANDY COUPON

This book is dedicated to all of my clients
and to my ex-wife
from whom I have learned so much
about the subject in these pages.

Special thanks are due to:

Jolene Jacobs
and the other divorce consultants
who have long served the public so well
and helped with the continuing updating
and improvement of this book.

and to
Trudy Ahlstrom
who keeps this operation going,

and to
Adrienne Chan-Sherman
who keeps me going.

Design and Graphics: Charles E. Sherman

PART ONE:

ALL ABOUT DIVORCE

CHAPTER

A

SOME BASIC INFORMATION ABOUT DIVORCE

The first thing you need to know is that the word "divorce" is technically incorrect. In California, as of 1970, the word was changed by law, so that marriages are dissolved and one now gets a dissolution, not a divorce. However, apart from legal usage, the word "divorce" is still the one everyone uses. It's hard to imagine someone getting fed up with their spouse and saying, "I'm going to dissolve you!" It just doesn't make it. But this book is about the legal process, so from now on we will call it "dissolution," and you can call it anything you like - outside of court.

Did you know that over 140,000 dissolutions are filed in California each year? And if you haven't already found it out, attorneys generally charge at least $400 and maybe $600 to handle simple, uncontested cases. This is in spite of the fact that they are really very easy to do. When this book first came out in 1971, less than 1% of all dissolutions were done without an attorney, but within a few years the picture changed entirely. Now 30% to 40% are done without a lawyer. That means that this book is saving Californians over $25 million every year in unnecessary legal fees. You can save a lot of money by doing it yourself, but there are many more advantages than that, as you will discover in this chapter.

A1 | *Can You Do Your Own Dissolution?*

Yes!

If you can read and understand this book, and if you can follow the clear and easy instructions in it, then you can do your own dissolution. As of 1981, over 500,000 people in California have had their marriages dissolved with this book, so you can probably do it too.

No!

There are only a few cases where you can **not** do your own dissolution without help. You should **not** do your own:

a) if your spouse hires an attorney and actually files legal papers to oppose you.

b) if your spouse is on **active** military duty **and** will **not** sign a waiver form.

Even if you feel that you cannot do your own dissolution, you should read this book because it will tell you all about your case - things most attorneys do not take the time to explain. It also gives you advice about how to get the best and most economical legal help.

Unless your case comes under one of the exceptions listed above, then you can almost certainly do your own dissolution. Read on!

A2 | *Deciding To Be Your Own Attorney*

The law says that it is your right to have an attorney represent you if you want one. **No** law says that you **must** have one. This book will help you to decide whether or not you need an attorney. In most dissolution cases, if there is no legal battle, you probably don't need an attorney. In fact, as you will learn below, there are big advantages to not having one.

In order to be your own attorney there must be no **legal** opposition from your spouse. Perhaps your spouse is long gone, or for some reason has no particular interest in what you may do. In such cases, you will probably have a very easy time of doing your own dissolution. Where your spouse **is** in the picture, **and** cares about what happens, you should talk things over and try to agree on basic things. There are important advantages to working things out (see A5, below). Also, being served with legal papers unexpectedly might send your spouse running to a lawyer and get you both involved in unnecessary legal tangles.

If you can't work things out, but you are not certain whether or not there will be actual **legal** opposition (maybe all that noise is just a bluff), you may decide to go ahead and start the case on your own. See what happens. If your spouse does get an attorney **and** file legal papers, then you will have to get an attorney, too.

Do not attempt to do your own dissolution if an uncooperative spouse is on **active** military duty. Either wait for him to get out, or get an attorney. However, if your military spouse will cooperate with you just to the extent of signing a paper which agrees to let the dissolution proceed, then there is a special procedure you can follow. It is called the Appearance and Waiver, and it is explained in Appendix A.

After you read all of the first part of this book, if you still have trouble understanding your case or making decisions, then you probably should get help. It may be that you can find an attorney who will charge by the hour for consultation to help you settle any confusions or undecided matters, then you can do the rest yourself.

If you start your own dissolution and run into trouble, you can always hire an attorney to get you out of it, so long as a judgment has not been finally rendered

---

A3 | *Advantages To Being Your Own Attorney*

a. IT'S MUCH CHEAPER TO DO IT YOURSELF

Perhaps the most obvious advantage to doing your own dissolution is the savings in cost. A State Bar survey in early 1982 reported fees ranging from $250 to $1500 for doing just a simple uncontested dissolution, with most falling between $400 and $700. Many attorneys said few cases stay uncontested! In almost every case where one spouse gets an attorney, the other spouse will get one too, and the cost will then be at least **double**.

In a few places in California there are legal clinics advertising low prices for simple uncontested dissolutions. If you happen to live near one, you may be able to find a lawyer who will do your case for as little as $250, plus court costs. The prices start out low, but can easily end up much higher before you are through (see next section). Even at full price, lawyers tend not to give you much time or information, and this is especially true in most cut-rate law offices. It may find it very difficult to get personal advice and attention. You almost always end up wondering what's going on, but there's no one to talk to about it.

Not all cut-rate lawyers operate this way. There are always those overworked and underpaid souls who are dedicated to counseling, education, and an ethical practice. They are rare. More about how to look for an attorney when you need one in Chapter A-11. The point here is that you save at least $250, more like $600, and as much as $1200 - $3000 by doing it yourself.

b. KEEPING IT SIMPLE

A lot of people start off with a simple case that doesn't necessarily end up that way. Lawyers have a way of making almost anything more complicated. This is because of the way they are trained, the way they think, and the way the system works. A lawyer is a combatant. Our system of justice is known as "the adversary system." It began on the medieval field of honor where trial by combat meant that whoever survived was right, and we see those same principles and attitudes in the courtrooms of today.

Law schools have **no** course requirement in counseling or communication skills. Instead, the training strongly emphasizes aggressive and defensive strategy and how to get the most financial advantage in every case. Is this the attitude you want in your dissolution?

Most dissolutions are fairly sensitive and it doesn't take much to stir them up. Your average attorney is just too likely to make things worse instead of better. Here's a typical example. Let's say that a couple is separated and they have things more or less stabilized in a situation where lots of sleeping dogs are being left to lie. Then one spouse goes to an attorney to start the dissolution. Often the attorney encourages the client to ask for more property and support than is actually expected. Lawyers think it pays to ask for extra so they can bargain their way back down. When the other spouse hears of this, it's a big shock, and that person will feel decieved. There's tension and trouble, not

to mention mistrust and hurt. In most cases, just receiving formal legal documents from an attorney will motivate the other spouse to go see their own attorney for an independent opinion. Then the fun really starts.

Two attorneys start off costing just double, but pretty soon they start writing letters and filing motions and doing standard attorney-type things, just like they were taught. Now we have a contested case, more fees and charges, and a couple of very upset spouses. Sure hope they don't have kids. The fees in contested cases can run from **a lot** all the way up to **everything**.

The moral of this story, and hundreds of thousands of others like it, is this: **If you do it yourself, there's a much better chance of keeping a simple case easy and simple.**

c. PERSONAL SATISFACTION

It's a bit more trouble if you do it yourself, but this way you will understand every step. You are completely in charge of your own case, your own decisions, and your own life.

This aspect of doing your own dissolution is subtle and often under-estimated, but it can generate the most important advantage of them all. Doing it yourself helps to overcome that helpless feeling that often comes at this time. It will focus your mind on the practical things, get you moving in a positive and constructive way, and give you a sense of movement out of the past and into your future. It feels good to stand on your own two feet.

A4 | *Making Decisions*

Part of the service you are supposed to get from a lawyer is help with making decisions about your affairs. They know which things have to be decided and they know the general standards and rules by which things are done in the courts. This is what the first part of this book is all about. It tells you what needs doing and the way things are generally done in cases where there is no fight. It gives you information and help with making your own decisions.

If, after reading this book, you can make your own decisions based on your own knowledge, then you probably do not need a lawyer. If you read this book and still have doubts or questions, then you probably should have professional advice. It may be that you can find an attorney who will help you settle your mind, then you can go on to do the rest on your own. Chapter A-11 tells you how to find such a person.

```
━━━━━━━━━ THINGS THAT MUST BE DECIDED ━━━━━━━━━

    • that the marriage should be ended forever, and
    • how to divide any property and bills that you may
  have accumulated during the marriage, and
    • if there is to be spousal support.
  Where there are no minor children, that's all there is to it. If
you have children, you must also decide:
    • who is to have custody of the children,
    • how visitation is to be arranged, and
    • how much is to be paid for child support.
```

As far as the law is concerned, this is what a dissolution is all about - settling the practical affairs of the couple and watching out for the well-being of the children. These are the things you must decide about in order to get a dissolution. **If** your spouse is in the picture **and** cares about what happens in the dissolution, then either you must be able to talk things over and come to some agreements, or you must be sure that your spouse will not get a lawyer and oppose you legally.

A5 | *Agreed and Default Dissolutions*

When a dissolution lawsuit is filed, it raises the issues outlined above. These issues can be resolved in one of only three ways: 1) by agreement of the parties, 2) by default, or 3) by contest. In the agreed case, the parties get together and settle the issues before going into court. In the default case, the Respondent is properly notified of the dissolution lawsuit, but does nothing about it legally, and no Response is filed. A person who does not show up for a contest loses by default. In the contested case, the Respondent files a Response and comes into court to do legal battle before a judge, who makes a decision in the case. You cannot do your own dissolution if a Response is filed.

a. THE DEFAULT DISSOLUTION

This kind of case is easy to do, assuming you can get papers served on your spouse. After a short wait you go in for a hearing and get your judgment. Even if your spouse barks, there is no bite so long as no Response is filed.

b. THE AGREED DIVORCE

If your spouse is in the picture **and** cares about what happens, then you should make efforts to reach an agreement on the legal issues of your dissolution. Look what you gain by having an agreement before you go through with your dissolution:

i) It is much easier, especially since you probably won't have to have papers served. This makes it faster, and a little cheaper, too.

ii) It is more certain as to how things will be ordered at the hearing. The judge will be very likely to follow the terms of any agreement that is not obviously unfair.

iii) It will help the Respondent feel better about letting the dissolution go through without contest or representation, since the terms of the order are pretty much settled ahead of time.

iv) It invariably leads to better relations with your ex-spouse. Where there are children, this is extremely important.

The agreed dissolution has so many big advantages that if there is any chance at all of working things out with your spouse, you should struggle for it.

c. TO FIGHT, OR NOT TO FIGHT - IS THAT THE QUESTION?

This is the point that divides the easy cases from the hard ones. The main reason for a difficult time with a dissolution is that the couple either wants to fight or just can't keep from it. Such people are angry or hurt and want to hurt back. They want to use the law as a weapon, to force their spouse into some sort of response. The law rarely has this result. Instead, it almost always turns a contested dissolution into a very unpleasant and very expensive failure. The dissolution will always go through, but no one will be happy about it. No one ever really wins a court battle.

If your case may turn into a fight, remember this: it is one thing to get an order against someone, but it is very much another thing to enforce that order. Especially in cases where there are children, a dissolution is not a final solution, since you have to deal with each other in the future because of the kids. In more ways than one, it really pays to work things out.

d. WORKING THINGS OUT

If you can't agree about basic things peacefully, maybe let some time pass. Wait to see if things settle down. It may be very helpful if you get another copy of this book, send it to your spouse, and then try to discuss various sections in it. This is a good idea because your spouse may misunderstand what a dissolution is about, and informed people are usually less emotional and irrational. It can get you talking about practical, constructive things. Also, the book helps to make these points:

☆ Fighting will not prevent the dissolution, it will only make it more unpleasant and much more expensive.

☆ Even contested dissolutions are decided according to the standards discussed in this book. Any monetary advantage gained by a fight is usually wiped out by the fees and costs of the battle. How do you value the emotional strain and future relations with your spouse and children?

If the reason you can't agree is emotional, or a basic inability to communicate, you can still be very successful if you can both agree to involve a third person. A trusted friend, a member of the clergy, or a professional mediator or counselor can often be very helpful at getting things worked out.

County Counseling Services: Many counties now have a Conciliation Court which provides marriage counseling for troubled marriages, either before or during a legal action. They would like to help you save your marriage, but they can also help you dissolve it more soundly and peacefully. Conferences with them are free, and their confidentiality is protected by law, so all you can lose is time. If you don't like their services, you can always go back to your legal proceeding.

Do not try to proceed with your own dissolution if you and your spouse are in such active and antagonistic opposition that your spouse is likely to get an attorney and fight you in court. If you are not certain what your spouse's attitude and response will be, whether your spouse will really oppose you or is just bluffing, then you can consider going ahead with your own dissolution. See what happens when your spouse is confronted with the reality of a court action. If your spouse gets an attorney to file response papers, then you must be ready to get one too. Always cover your bets.

A6 | *Dissolution, Nullity, Separate Maintenance*

If you take an unhappy marriage into court, there are three ways the law can be used to end things: dissolution, nullity, and separate maintenance. In any of these, the court is able to make orders regarding child custody, support, and property. The differences between them are mostly theoretical and the practical differences are, for most purposes, relatively minor.

An order for separate maintenance gets the spouses separated and makes orders about children, support and property, but it leaves the parties still married. This law is used mostly where there are religious or moral reasons for not wanting to end the marriage, but yet the spouses want to live apart. Sometimes the reason is economic, such as where there are big tax advantages, or sizeable retirement, Veteran's, Social Security, or other benefits to be lost in case of dissolution. It is quite legal for spouses to separate without courts or lawyers simply by moving apart, but then they must get along without court orders. This book does not show you how to do a separate maintenance.

A nullity (formerly called annulment) declares that the marriage in question never existed, while a dissolution says that the marriage will cease to exist at the end of the dissolution. Both have the same effect, to restore the parties to the status of single persons, but the nullity permits you to remarry immediately after the hearing, while the dissolution makes you wait a few months longer. The dissolution has a residency requirement (see below) while the others do not. Most other differences are mostly theoretical. Since the grounds for nullity are more complicated than for a dissolution, and since courts tend to be more strict in nullity cases, it is therefore recommended that you do not try to do your own nullity. This book does not show you how to get one.

A dissolution will almost always serve your purposes as well as any of the other forms, but if you want a separate maintenance or a nullity, see an attorney.

Summary Dissolution: In 1979, California created a second way to do a dissolution. The way we have always done it is called **Regular Dissolution**, and the new method, which is simpler but more limited, is called **Summary Dissolution**. The only difference between them is the way they are done, but the effect in either case is the same. The two are compared in detail in Chapter F.

A7 | *Grounds for Dissolution*

The main ground for dissolution in California is "Irreconcilable Differences." In a Regular Dissolution you are also allowed to use grounds of "Incurable Insanity." Incurable Insanity refers to people who are medically, scientifically crazy. Your spouse may seem weird to you, or even dangerous, but that may not be enough. The insanity case is too complicated for you to present without an attorney, but if your spouse is "different" you can definitely go ahead and use the grounds of Irreconcilable Differences.

You have Irreconcilable Differences when there is some substantial reason for not continuing the marriage, and so serious that you are sure there can be no reconciliation. Nearly all marriages are now terminated on these grounds. If your marriage is ending for any serious reason, you probably fit the description. It is only theoretically possible for a court to refuse the dissolution because your reasons are not good enough, but in practice this is unheard of.

A8 | *Residency Requirements*

Your residence in California is what gives the court power to dissolve your marriage. No matter where you were married, some other state or some other country, if you meet the residency requirement, you can be divorced in California.

Both the Regular Dissolution and the Summary Dissolution have the same residency requirement: either you or your spouse must have lived in California for at least six months, and in the county where you file your papers for at least three months, just prior to filing the Petition. Being away temporarily, as on a business trip or vacation, does not count against your residency time. After you file your Petition there is no more requirement for residency, so you can move anywhere you wish.

A9 | *Notice to Your Spouse*

In our system, a lawsuit is regarded as a struggle between two contestants conducted before an impartial authority (the judge). The one who is most "right" wins. It seems obvious (doesn't it?) that you can't have a fair contest if the other side doesn't even know one is going on. The essence of notice is that your spouse gets a Summons and a copy of your Petition, and so can be presumed to know what the suit is about, what you want, and when and where the contest is to be held. The court cannot act in your case unless you can properly notify your spouse of the lawsuit. Chapter 8 shows how this is done.

The need for proper notice is especially obvious in cases which go by default, which is what happens when your spouse gets proper notice and does nothing. A person who fails to show up at a contest loses by default. Since your spouse has received the Petition and knows what is in it and what you are asking, not showing up is one way of saying that you can have your way. Subject to the judge's approval, that is what you will get.

A10 Required Waiting Periods

In case you might cool off and reconcile, California law has imposed a required waiting period. In a Summary Dissolution you cannot file for the final judgment until six months after the date you filed the Petition. In a Regular Dissolution you cannot file final papers until at least six months after the date of service of the first papers on your spouse. You are not legally divorced until the final judgment is ordered and entered in the clerk's records.

In Regular Dissolutions there is also a waiting period of 60 days following the hearing to allow for possible appeals, during which time you cannot request the final judgment. If your hearing is held within four months of service of process, then by the time the six month waiting period is up, the 60 day appeal period will also be over.

A11 *How to Find the Right Attorney*

If you have trouble with some part of doing your own dissolution, or if you and your spouse are trying to work out terms and get stuck, or if you need more information or legal advice, or for any other reason at all, you may decide that a little time spent in conference with an attorney would be worthwhile. Instead of having an attorney do the whole job, you might just get help with part of it. Some attorneys may not be willing to do this, but you can find out quickly by telephone.

Shopping for an attorney is very much like shopping for melons. You not only have to check the prices, but you also have to smell them and squeeze them to see if they "feel" right to you. We obviously don't mean for you to go around squeezing and smelling attorneys, but you have a right to ask questions, look things over, and be choosy about whom you hire. There really are some good, honest lawyers around, but you have to search them out.

The best way to find an attorney is through some friend or trusted person who has had a satisfactory personal experience with one. But don't forget to check things out for yourself. Don't be intimidated. Call around on the telephone to find out how much an initial interview will cost, and how much the whole job might cost. See if you like the way the attorney and the law office staff treat you. Talk to them. If you only want some advice as part of doing your own dissolution, ask ahead of time to see if they are willing to do this and find out how what their rates are for consultations. Most attorneys will do the first interview for a fairly small fee, perhaps $15 to $20. Hourly rates run from $20 to $200 per hour, but $40 is fairly common. Price is not everything —it has to feel right. Talk to the attorney and see if you like the experience.

If you belong to a union or work for a large organization, they may have a company lawyer that will be able to help you, especially if it's just advice. Some areas have group legal service plans open to the public, such as the excellent Consumer's Group Legal Service which operates throughout the San Francisco Bay Area.

Before you go in to see an attorney, be sure you are thoroughly prepared in your own case and know exactly what you want from the attorney. Have all the relevant documents and information with you when you go in.

A12 Some Common Questions and Answers

a) **How much will it cost to do my own dissolution?** The filing fees are set from time to time by law. As of 1981, it costs about $90 to file your papers in the typical default case. If you decide to file the Appearance & Waiver form signed by your spouse (see Appendix A), it will cost an additional $70. Other ways of serving notice on your spouse can often be accomplished for free or cheap. Add to this a few dollars for Xerox copies and postage, and that's it. If you hired an attorney, these charges would be added to the fee, so you will be paying them in any event.

b) **How long will it take?** The shortest possible time to complete a divorce is six months from the service of notice on your spouse. It is okay to take longer.

c) **What if we reconcile?** When you apply for your final judgment, you must swear that you have not reconciled or agreed to dismiss the action.

Reconciliation is a state of mind which goes beyond merely dating or occasionally sleeping together. Actually living together for a period of time might require some clever explaining if you deny that it was a reconciliation. If you do not intend to complete your dissolution, you should file a dismissal form. Send $3 to Nolo Press for the form and instructions.

d) **When can we remarry?** After your final decree of dissolution is ordered **and** entered in the Clerk's record books, you are immediately free to remarry. It is quite all right to wait longer. Take your time.

e) **What if the wife is pregnant?** An unborn child of the spouses **must** be mentioned in the Petition. Any child born to a married woman is presumed to be that of the husband. If they were cohabiting when it was conceived, and if the husband was not medically impotent or sterile, then the presumption is just short of conclusive. If there is or may be a dispute as to paternity, you had better see an attorney.

f) **Am I entitled to my spouse's income after separation?** No. After separation, the income and accumulations of either spouse are their own separate property, so long as the spouses live apart and do not intend to reunite, whether or not any legal action has been filed.

g) **Am I liable for my spouse's bills incurred after separation?** Generally, no, but only if you are careful to close all joint accounts, cancel joint credit cards, and notify any creditors that are accustomed to extending credit to you jointly.

h) **Does divorce have tax consequences?** Yes. Almost every aspect of divorce could **possibly** have important tax consequences. The tax rules are numerous and change frequently, but fortunately there is an excellent and free little booklet which clearly tells you everything you will want to know. Call your local Internal Revenue Service office and ask for IRS publication 504, "Tax Information for Divorced or Separated Individuals."

26   DIVIDING THE PROPERTY

CHAPTER

B

DIVIDING THE PROPERTY AND BILLS

One of the central parts of a dissolution is dividing the estate - the property and debts of the marriage. One of the most important services of an attorney is going over your estate with you to see what you own, what you owe, and how it can all be divided. This book will tell you how to understand your own estate and decide for yourself how to divide it.

B1 Cases Where There Is No Property

Do not conclude that you have no property without carefully going over the Property Declaration in Chapter 11. Use it as a check list to make sure that you have thought of everything, especially pension plans, which many people forget to look into.

Cases without property are very easy to do because you merely tell the court that there is no significant property to be divided, and the court does nothing. There will be little inquiry into your property and no orders about it.

Several different kinds of cases can be handled this simple way. It may be that there is not enough property to worry about, where you own little more than your few personal possessions. Or maybe your spouse is long gone, doesn't care, or has abandoned what little property there is to you. Or maybe you and

---

your spouse have already divided things between you, so at the time you file your suit there is nothing left to be divided by the court. In cases like these, you may decide that you do not need or want the court to become involved with making orders about the division of your property.

Do not take this approach if there is any chance of a future argument about property of any significant value, or where there is real estate that has not yet been divided correctly, or where there is a community interest in a pension plan.

B2 | *Cases Where There Is Some Property*

Make sure you understand your estate and know **all** that it contains. Read Chapter B3 and go over the Property Declaration in Chapter 11 very carefully to make sure you have thought of everything (this is the kind of check list attorneys use). If you think it likely that your spouse has hidden assets that you don't know and can't find out about, then you may benefit from the services of an attorney. An attorney can get the spouse in court and under order to reveal everything.

If at the time of your dissolution the community estate contains property or bills of any significant value, then you will want to have things divided properly as part of the dissolution.

Property can be divided by the parties or by the judge. Spouses can agree to divide their property any way they see fit. If this is completed before the Petition is filed, then there is no community property to divide and the case will be very easy to conduct. If there is some community property, but no agreement at the time of filing, then the property **must** be listed in the Petition. If by the time of the court hearing there is still no agreement, the property will be divided by the judge. In this case, neither spouse will be entirely in command of how the property gets divided, although the judge will be strongly influenced by the suggestions of the Petition or the spouse in court.

When thinking about dividing your property, keep in mind that getting the last cent may not be your best or highest goal. Consider the children, if any, the relative earning ability of each of you, your general situation, fairness and other such things. Try to consider what will be best for everyone, both now and in the future.

If you have a lot of property, you might want to think about getting professional advice from an accountant or lawyer. How much is "a lot" is up to you, and depends in part on how concerned you are about whatever you happen to have. A professional can tell you how to locate it, value it, divide it, transfer it, and generally protect your interests. Dividing property might have tax consequences, depending upon how much you have and how you do it. Study the pamphlet described in Chapter A12h and/or consider getting advice from a tax expert.

B3 | *Understanding Your Estate*

a) COMMUNITY AND SEPARATE PROPERTY DEFINED

Only your community property needs to be divided, since separate property already belongs to each spouse individually. In many cases, however, it makes good sense to list specially those items you wish to have clearly characterized as separate. This will make things more clear in the future. This listing is done either in a written agreement between the spouses or in your Petition. If listed in the Petition, by not filing a Response your spouse is accepting your list.

Separate Property belongs just to one spouse and not the community. Separate property is:
  • property that was acquired before the marriage; or
  • property that at **any** time came directly to just one
      spouse by gift or inheritance.
After the separation, the earnings, accumulations, and bills of each spouse are separate.

Community Property belongs to both spouses equally. Community property is anything acquired by either spouse during the marriage that is not separate property. This includes the negative property - bills - which either spouse incurred up to the time of separation. Don't forget about accumulated vacation pay, pension funds, tax refunds, and equity in insurance policies which may have been accumulated during the marriage.

You will see the term **quasi-community property** on the Petition and Property Declaration forms. This refers to property acquired by the spouses in another state before residency in California which would be community property if it had been acquired in California. It is treated the same as community property, but must be identified separately on the form.

Separate property can be changed into community property by agreement or intention of the owner-spouse. The agreement need not be in writing, and can even be inferred from conduct in some cases. For example, separate money used to purchase or improve a family home which is jointly held is presumed to be a gift to the community unless there is a clear agreement that it is to remain separate. Similarly, community property can be changed to the separate property of one spouse, but this takes the intention or agreement of both spouses, since both are owners of the community property. Without some clear agreement, separate property that is mixed up and mingled with community property tends to become community property. A written agreement **is** required to change the separate property of one spouse into separate property of the other. There is more on the subject of marital property in Nolo's book, California Marriage and Divorce Law (see inside back cover).

If your estate is tangled, complicated, or in any way difficult for you to understand and deal with, then consider consulting an attorney for advice on just this one point alone. Once things are straightened out, perhaps you can still proceed with your own dissolution.

b) BILLS AND LIABILITIES OF THE SPOUSES

If there are bills owed by you and your spouse that were accumulated during your marriage, then they will have to be valued and divided along with the property.

One thing you must understand is that orders of the court and agreements between the spouses about who is to pay bills do not in any way affect the people you owe. If you owed money to someone before the dissolution, and if your spouse is ordered to pay the bill but does not do it, then **you** still owe the money. The creditor can come after you and/or repossess the property. Your spouse may be in contempt of court, for all the good that does you.

If you are especially burdened by bills or being harassed by creditors, Nolo Press offers two books which may help you: "Billpayer's Rights," and "Bankruptcy - Do It Yourself" (see inside back cover).

As soon as you separate, close all joint accounts and notify all creditors in writing, preferably by certified mail, return receipt requested. Thereafter, under most circumstances, you will not be liable for the future debts of your spouse.

c) PENSION AND RETIREMENT PLANS

If the community has a share of any kind of retirement plan, it **must** be dealt with as part of the dissolution. Judges are interested in this subject and are likely to bring it up at the hearing even if you don't. Let's surprise them and be prepared!

This area can be a real can of worms. If you read through the material below and get confused, don't feel bad, because it confuses lawyers just as much as it does you. Push through to the end where we make some practical suggestions about how to deal with your community interest in a pension plan.

Does the community have an interest in a pension plan? If either spouse is now covered by a pension plan and was a member of that plan during the marriage, then some part of that plan is community property. **The community share** is the number of married years the spouse was part of the plan, divided by the total number of years of service at the time payments first become payable, and you are entitled to half of the community share. You must try to estimate the **current** worth of the community interest. **Note well:** what seems like little or nothing now could mean a great deal to you in the future, especially over a period of time after retirement.

Social Security, Military Pensions, Federal Pensions: Social Security is **not** community property and not subject to division by a court. It is a federal program with its own rules, so contact the Social Security Administration about your rights after divorce. Civil Service retirement benefits are subject to adjudication in state courts, and military retirement pay is subject to attachment in the enforcement of **support** orders. As of February, 1983, military retired pay or retainer pay **may** be treated as community property in state courts. If a least 20 years was served during the marriage, the ex-spouse can continue to receive health benefits and PX privileges. Military active pay is probably not community property, but the issue is not decided. The military pay area is tangled, so if your case is stumbling on this issue, either work something out between you by agreement, or plan to see an attorney and spend the rest of your days in litigation.

What is the community interest worth? The many different pension plans have one thing in common -- they can be extremely difficult to value before payments are actually due. In most cases the employee has paid in some amount which is payable at any time upon termination, and this amount will be easy to determine. However, the employer's contributions are generally payable in the form of pension payments which are due only if and when the employee works through to retirement age. At the time of your dissolution, the retirement fund may be unvested, immature, and contingent, thus making it extremely tricky to value, yet it must be dealt with at this time.

Precise and correct valuation of the present value of a future pension right is best done by a professional actuary who specializes in pensions, but there are hardly any of these around. Most lawyers would not be capable of doing it right, nor would most accountants. It is not certain that anyone can. Most cases, therefore, even with lawyers handling them, are done by general rule-of-thumb estimates of value. One thing you can do on your own is write to the officer of the union or company that manages the plan and ask for details about how the plan works, dates of the employee's participation, amount of employer contribution, amounts due to the employee in the event of immediate termination, and their estimate of the current worth of the plan. The community share is the ratio described above, and each spouse is entitled to half of the community share.

If you think the pension plan may be of significant value or importance to you, you may want to call various accountants in your area to try to find one that seems to know something about the valuation of pension plans. Get help on just this one point. An exact valuation may be unnecessary, depending upon how you decide to deal with it.

How to deal with it: Here are two ways you can deal with a community interest in a pension plan. There are undoubtedly other ways, but they are not covered here.

i) Trade-off or waiver: By this method, the employee spouse gets the half of the community share to which the non-employee spouse is entitled, thus having it all, and the non-employee spouse gets some other community property of a value equal to the share that was given up, or maybe a promissory note (due on a certain date, or when and if benefits become payable). If there is not enough other community property for a trade-off, and if no note is exchanged, then the non-employee spouse might just waive (give up) all interest in exchange for good will or nothing at all.

The Petitioner can make an oral waiver at the hearing, but at an uncontested hearing the Respondent does not appear, so any waiver from Respondent must be part of a written agreement (Chapter E) or in the form of a written waiver to be presented at the hearing by the Petitioner. It should say something like: "I, _____, am fully aware that there is or may be a community interest in my spouse's pension plan #A5S22A at Wahoo Corp, Cerritos, CA. After giving it careful thought I have decided that I do not need nor want any part of it. I hereby waive any and all right which I may have to said pension plan. (Signed)(Date)." Although not necessary, having it notarized would have good effect.

ii) Put it off: Another way to deal with a pension is to ask the judge to reserve jurisdiction to fix the rights of the parties at some time in the future. If and when the employee-spouse first gets the right to retire and collect benefits, the whole matter becomes much more clear and easier to deal with. At this time, either spouse can come back into court with a motion to have the matter settled.

Note: If a pension plan is not completely settled at the time of the dissolution - that is, if anything is left to be paid out of the plan in the future - then a lawyer would be sure to join the pension plan as a party in your dissolution and get the judge to order that it never make payments without notifying you first. This is the safest way, but too complicated for you to do on your own. We suggest instead that you have the judge order the employee-spouse not to apply for or accept benefits without first notifying the other spouse **and** applying to the court for a determination and division of community interest in the plan.

If you feel that you have a right in a pension plan that might be worth protecting beyond the methods we have described here, then you should consult an attorney.

If after reading this section, you are still uncertain about your rights or what to do, then you should see an attorney or CPA, at least for advice. The problem is that a great many professionals don't know much about it either. Ask before you go in.

e) THE FAMILY HOME AND OTHER REAL ESTATE

If you and your spouse own or have been buying your own home or other real property at the time of the dissolution, then you must decide how to divide it. Some of the likely alternatives are to:
- sell it and split the proceeds, or
- have one spouse transfer it outright to the other, or
- have one spouse transfer it to the other in return for something, such as other property, or a note for some amount to be paid in the future (at some specific date or upon some specified event, such as when the kids are grown, if and when the house is sold, the spouse moves out of it, or any other determinable time that you can agree to).

Your dissolution will be much easier if you can settle the matter of the real estate and transfer it before you file the Petition. That way you won't have to list the house and make orders about it. Agreements about real property are **not** enforceable unless they are in writing.

If there are children living in a long-established family home, judges are reluctant to force a sale of the house, and if a sale would cause economic, emotional, or social detriment to the kids, the judge is **required** to defer the sale, unless the economic detriment to the non-custodial spouse would outweigh the other considerations.

When thinking about what to do with your family home or other real property, you will want to know how much of it you actually own. This amount is called your "equity." Your equity in any property is the difference between what you can get for it on the current market less the amount(s) due on it and less the cost of selling it. You can find out the current market value of your property by consulting a professional real estate appraiser. This will cost some money, so call around for prices. You could also call in a few local real estate agents, but this would not be as reliable. Once you have figured the market value, deduct the amounts you owe on it and the commission for the real estate agents, about 6 or 8%. There would also be miscellaneous expenses of a few hundred dollars. The amount left over is your equity. Assuming the house was held by both spouses jointly, and acquired during the marriage, the entire amount is community property, and each spouse is entitled to half.

If you make a written agreement with your spouse about your real property, you must then transfer title from one to the other. To transfer real property from joint ownership by both spouses into sole ownership of one spouse, you need to make up a deed from one spouse to the other, then have that deed signed before a Notary and recorded at the County Recorder's Office in the county where the property is located. Similarly, if a note is to be taken back, then it too must be properly drawn up, signed, and recorded together with a Deed of Trust. There will be a small fee for recordation and maybe a transfer tax. If you cannot make up your own deed or note from forms available at a stationary store, then you should seek assistance from a title company, a bank, a real estate broker, or an attorney. Call around to see what they will charge you.

If you do not transfer the home before the Petition is filed, then it must be disposed of in a marital settlement agreement or listed with your other property as shown in Chapter 6. If it is still not transferred by the time of the hearing, or settled by written agreement of the spouses, then the judge will divide it along with all the other listed property. When you prepare the Interlocutory Judgment (Chapter 13), use the full legal description of the house exactly as it appears on your deed (you can get a copy from the County Recorder). If your house is in California, get a certified copy of the Interlocutory Judgment and take it to the County Recorder for the county where the house is located and have it recorded. This makes the Judgment effective as a transfer of title to the house.

The time and manner of transfer could easily have tax consequences such that it would benefit both spouses to cooperate over the transfer to arrange it to their own advantage. See Chapter A12h and/or a tax expert.

If, after reading this, you still have trouble dealing with your real property - how to value it, divide it, or transfer it - it may be best if you consult an attorney, at least on this one point.

B4 | *When Property Is Divided by the Court*

If at the time of your dissolution there is any significant community property or debts, it must be properly divided. Community property can be divided either by agreement of the spouses, or by the court according to legal standards. There are many advantages to working things out by agreement (discussed above in A5), but it will help if you know how things work if left to the court to divide.

Property divided by the court will be divided in half, so that each spouse gets equal value. This will usually be done according to some plan presented by the Petitioner.

Where there are children, it is often fair to leave more of the property with the spouse maintaining custody. Judges are usually willing to keep the family home and most of the household goods together to maintain comfort and stability for the children (see discussion in B3d, above). This means that the spouse that does not have the children will sometimes have to wait for his/her share of the community property until the kids grow up, become emancipated, the family moves, or the like.

If your spouse cannot be located after diligent search, and if the value of the community property is under $5,000, then it is possible to have it all awarded to you. Be prepared to prove that your search was complete and thorough (see Appendix D).

If the court awards you property that is still in the possession of your spouse, you still have to figure out how to get it. If you can't get it peacefully, then you'll need to hire an attorney, if the property is worth the money and trouble.

B5 | *Dividing It By Agreement*

If your property is minimal, then you can just go ahead and divide it up, and that will be that. Where there are items of any value, it is usually better to make some sort of written agreement just to help you keep track of what it was you actually agreed to. If there is any real estate, then the agreement **must** be in writing. If the Respondent is to give up rights to a pension plan or spousal support, there must be a written agreement or a written waiver to show the judge.

In uncontested dissolutions, a judge will nearly always follow the agreement of the spouses, so long as it appears to be generally fair. But you should know that the judge is not legally bound to follow your agreement on matters of child custody, support, and visitation. For example, few judges would allow a welfare mother to waive spousal support, nor agree to an unreasonably low amount for child support, even if she wanted to.

Chapter E discusses written agreements and shows you two ways to go about making one.

B6 | *Wills*

A dissolution does **not** have any effect on any will already in existence. If you want to change the terms of your will to cut out your ex-spouse, you will have to write a new will.

CHAPTER C

CHILDREN: CUSTODY AND VISITATION

C1 | *Generally*

If there are children, the court will want to make orders about their custody and support. The court is only concerned with minor children born naturally to both parents or adopted by the stepparent. If the wife is pregnant, that child must also be mentioned in the Petition as "one unborn."

If you have children, the dissolution does not completely end the relationship between you and your spouse. Although you no longer live together, chances are that you will see one another from time to time about matters concerning the children, and to permit visitation. Since your relationship will probably continue, try to keep things as pleasant as possible - it is not good for either of you or for the children if you can't get over your differences, at least enough to permit the parental relationship to continue and to grow.

There is only one test used for making decisions concerning children: "What is in the child's best interest?" This is the question asked by the law, judges, and most parents. It's the question you and your spouse should ask.

All orders concerning child custody, visitation, and support are subject to modification. If circumstances change, either parent can go back into court at any time and seek a change in the court orders.

C2 Custody

When one parent gets custody of the children, that person has the major responsibility of caring for, housing, and raising them. This person also has the last word on all matters concerning their upbringing.

Until recently, joint custody was not much favored by judges. It was felt that if a couple got along badly managing their own lives, they could not be expected to work smoothly and peacefully together at raising their children. But you may have noticed that times are changing, and the lawmakers have noticed it too. Effective January, 1980, there is a new law setting priorities for custody.

Custody is awarded according to the best interest of the child, in the following order of preference:

1. To either parent, or both parents jointly, without any preference to a parent because of that parent's sex.

Joint custody is **presumed** to be best if the parents have agreed to it. The judge **may** require the parents to present a plan showing how their arrangement would work in practice. In counties with a Conciliation Court, the parents can use the counselors to help make up their plan or to work out differences under it.

The judge has discretion to award joint custody upon request of one parent if it seems best for the child(ren). On request of either party, the judge can order a family study to assist the judge in making a decision.

2. To the person(s) in whose home the child has been living in a wholesome and stable environment.

3. When the child is old enough to reason and make intelligent choices, then the judge will give weight to the desires of the child.

4. All matters concerning custody are subject to modification in the future, to serve the best interest of the child(ren).

If your award is for joint custody, pure and simple, then you will have accomplished the progressive intention of the law, and both parents will continue to have equal and complete parental power and authority just as before the dissolution. However, the law gives the judge discretion to order joint **legal** custody without ordering joint **physical** custody. A split joint custody order might read, "Joint legal custody to A and B, with primary physical custody to A," and maybe visitation for B. When this is done, it sounds nice, but that's almost its only advantage. Split joint custody looses the desired effect, and worse, exactly what it does mean is unclear and untested. It is **probably** very much like the old-style award of custody to one and visitation to the other parent, with a bit more legal power for the non-custodial parent (power to order medical care, consent to minor's marriage, and the like), but no one can be sure just yet.

When there is no contest between parents about who is to have custody, the court will almost always make the award requested by Petitioner. If you and your spouse are having difficulty communicating or working out custody and visitation, then it is strongly recommended that you seek help, advice, and counseling. Court fights over custody are almost always destructive, especially to the child(ren).

If your spouse takes legal action to contest your choices for custody, then it is obvious that you cannot do your own dissolution, and you must get legal assistance.

C3 Visitation

The parent that does not get custody is almost always given the "right of reasonable visitation." This means that subject to the approval of the parent having custody, the other parent is entitled to visit at reasonable times and places, upon reasonable notice. It is left to the parents to work out their own relationship and plans for visits. It is hoped that both will keep the best interests of the child uppermost, and work toward creating as open and flexible an atmosphere as possible to permit a happy and growing relationship between the child and the visiting parent. In addition to flexibility, try to approach regularity and consistency - this is good for all parties, especially the children. Occasional extended visits and trips away ought to be possible.

Sometimes the communication between the parents is so broken down and full of conflict that they will be unlikely to work out their own visitation arrangements in any flexible manner. In such cases, if you can show the court that there is a good reason for doing so, a regular schedule can be ordered setting out specific days and hours for visiting. Courts tend to order that visits be permitted on one or two days of the week, or every other week. Depending upon the circumstances, particularly the age of the child, over-night visits and extended vacation visits may or may not be ordered. If your spouse has a history of harassing and annoying you, visiting can be ordered away from your home, possibly by arrangement through third persons.

The relationship between parent and child is so respected and protected that courts almost never order that there be no visiting permitted at all. In fact, there are criminal sanctions against any parent who keeps or conceals a child in order to frustrate custody or visitation orders. In order to obtain an order preventing all visits you would have to make a strong and clear showing that visits would be very detrimental or dangerous to the child. You might, however, get an order for visits only in the presence of an approved third party. If you feel you need to **prevent** visiting by court order you would be better off with an attorney.

The parent with custody is not entitled to forbid visiting for any reason other than the well-being of the children. If the visiting spouse shows up in a drugged, drunken, or highly emotional condition, it would be reasonable to prevent the visit on that occasion. However, according to the law, visiting cannot be refused because of a disagreement or ill-will between the parents, or even because of a complete failure to provide support.

Once you have your custody and visitation order, it is hoped that all will go smoothly. If not, and if you can't work things out on a personal level, you should try counseling (see Chapter A5d). In extreme cases, a lawyer may be needed to enforce the order.

CHAPTER
D

SUPPORT

The obligation of the parent to support the child is natural, basic, and enforced by law. It has the highest priority for attention and concern, both in law and in the minds of judges. The duty lasts during the minority of the child or until the child dies, marries, or becomes emancipated (self-supporting). Californians become adults at age 18, so court orders for child support are effective until the child's 18th birthday. Support can be ordered extended to age 21 only if agreed to by both parties (see Chapter E).

Spousal support is second in priority to child support. In many families, once adequate child support is ordered there often isn't much left over for more than token spousal support. When thinking about spousal support, it is very important to consider the length of the marriage and the earning ability of the spouses. Alimony is not favored much where the marriage is very short, or where there are no children and both spouses can take care of themselves. This differs from case to case and judge to judge. Given the right circumstances of earnings and need, it is possible for the wife to be ordered to support the husband, although this is relatively uncommon.

The amount of support to be paid for the children and/or for the spouse is determined by a consideration of such things as:

Standard of living of the parties,
Relative income of the parties,
Earning ability of the parties,
Needs of each party and the children,
Ages of the parties and the children, and
Responsibility for the support of others.

In other words, the courts will balance the needs of one against the ability to pay of the other and come up with something that is supposed to be reasonable. The question of support is very difficult to treat in any specific way, since everything depends upon the particular circumstances of your own case.

Many county agencies have prepared guidelines for child and spousal support, but these vary widely from county to county and agency to agency. Just for example, the next two pages show the schedules used by the judges in Marin County as a guideline for their support orders. **CAUTION**: this is only a very general guide which is also out of date. Because of inflation, this guide may be a little low, especially for upper income groups. It should not be used without consideration of all factors. Make up your own mind, based upon your own situation. The first schedule covers child support, and the second covers spousal support. Add them together if you have children.

SCHEDULE FOR CHILD SUPPORT PAYMENTS
WHERE NO SPOUSAL SUPPORT IS ORDERED

Non-custodial Parent's Net Monthly Income**	One Child	Two Children	Three or More Children
$ 400.00	$ 100.00	$ 100.00	$ 100.00
500.00	125.00	150.00	175.00
600.00	150.00	200.00	225.00
700.00	150.00	250.00	275.00
800.00	150.00	250.00	300.00
900.00	175.00	275.00	350.00
1000.00	175.00	300.00	375.00
1200.00	200.00	350.00	450.00
1400.00	250.00	400.00	525.00
1600.00	250.00	450.00	600.00
1800.00	275.00	500.00	675.00
2000.00	300.00	550.00	750.00
Above 2000.00	Court's discretion		

NOTE:

This schedule is prepared with the assumption that the custodial parent's net earnings are at least 25% less than that of the non-custodial parent, and that there is no award of spousal support.

The rule for support is intended to be the same whether the custodial parent is the father or the mother.

If the non-custodial parent carries hospital, medical or dental insurance covering the children, the cost attributable to the children's coverage may be deducted from the support payments.

**Income after compulsory deductions such as income tax, FICA, SDI and compulsory retirement.

GUIDE LINES FOR DURATION OF SPOUSAL SUPPORT
AFTER DISSOLUTION OR LEGAL SEPARATION

LENGTH OF MARRIAGE	DURATION OF SUPPORT
Under 12 years	It is presumed that spousal support shall terminate after a period equivalent to one-half the duration of the marriage.
12 to 25 years	There is no presumption for termination of spousal support. The following factors to be considered (whether or note it shall terminate): wife's education, training, work experience, health and age; husband's ability to pay support; wife's eligibility for social security.*
Over 25 years	It is presumed that permanent spousal support shall not terminate unless wife remarries.

1. Presence or absence of preschool children to be considered if husband has income above minimum.

2. Special consideration to be given to the ill health of either spouse.

3. After 25 years of marriage, the wife is presumed to require spousal support.

4. Duration of temporary spousal support payments should be taken into account.

*Current Social Security Regulations (42 U.S.C. 402b) provide that a wife divorced after 10 years of marriage is entitled to social security benefits.

AMOUNT OF SPOUSAL SUPPORT

If the *net* earnings of one spouse are $300.00 to $600.00, *maximum* support to the other spouse is ⅓ of that income.

If the *net* earnings of one spouse are over $600.00, *maximum* support to the other spouse shall not exceed 40% of that amount.

If there is both spousal and child support, the combined order should not exceed 50% of the supporting spouse's net income.

No spousal support shall be provided to any spouse who, following dissolution, has income sufficient to maintain his or her standard of living.

If you have trouble making decisions or agreeing about support, consider seeing a counselor (see A5d) or an attorney (see A-11) to help you come to some reasonable conclusions. Another solution is to just let the judge decide it. At the time of the hearing, tell the judge that you are asking for "reasonable support" for your child and/or yourself, and that you want him to apply his own experience and standards to the case. Be prepared to state a range for what you think is fair in case he asks it for his own information.

If there are children, the court will be concerned to see that adequate arrangements have been made for their support. Petitioners with children **must** check box 7(b) on the Petition and include an order for child support in the Interlocutory Judgment. As long as you are not on welfare, the court will probably let you determine the amount of support to be ordered. The judge will worry only if it seems too high or too low, but since the case is uncontested it will probably go according to your choice.

Spousal support is forever waived (given up) if not claimed at the outset. An order for spousal support can be modified in the future if circumstances of need or ability to pay should change, but where there is a written agreement for spousal support, the parties can specifically agree that the amount cannot be modified. If Petitioner is the wife and she does not wish to give up her right to support, she should claim at least a token amount, say $1 per month. This leaves open the possibility for coming back to court later. If Petitioner is the husband, there will have to be at least a token award of spousal support unless he can bring in a written waiver signed by the wife. The waiver should read something like this:

> I, _____, am the Respondent in a dissolution proceeding being conducted by default. After careful consideration, it is my desire to waive all right now and for the future to spousal support. I understand that by making this waiver now, I am forever giving up whatever rights I may have to spousal support.
> Date: Signed: _____

Jurisdiction: In order for the court to make an enforceable order for payment of money against any person, there has to be "personal" jurisdiction. This usually means that person must be served personally inside California, or sign the Appearance and Waiver (Appendix A). If your spouse cannot be served in California, and if you want a judgment for money, you should use the Appearance and Waiver. If your spouse will not sign it, go ahead with other types of service, but the validity of your money judgment depends upon obscure legal points such as "minimum contacts." You can probably get a judgment for support, but it may or may not be enforceable if your spouse raises a legal challenge later. You may want to see an attorney on this point.

Enforcement: When support is ordered it still remains to be collected. If your spouse doesn't pay what is ordered, you will probably need professional help to collect it. He can be brought into court for contempt of court, or sued for breach of contract (if he signed a written agreement), or have his wages attached, etc. The mere fact that you have a support order does not always mean you will get the money. If child support is involved, your District Attorney will help you collect back child **and** spousal support, free of charge. Some DA's offices are very good and some are not. Ask around.

Welfare cases: California law requires that in any case where child support is ordered for a person receiving welfare for the support of minor children, the support **must** be paid through an office of the court. Ask your County Clerk who they use in your county to receive these payments.

Taxes: Child support is not taxable, but spousal support is. The person paying spousal support can deduct such payments, and the recipient **must** report it as a taxable income. In some cases the spouses may be able to save money by juggling these categories. Income tax exemptions are allowed for children, but when the parents are divorced, they cannot both claim the same child as a dependent. The rules for who can claim the child as an exemption are, as you might guess, intricate and subject to change, but here is one very important general rule: it is very much to the advantage of the **non**custodial parent to have the decree or a written agreement specify who may claim the child as a dependent. Without such written order or agreement, the noncustodial parent cannot claim any child as an exemption unless more than $1200 is paid during the year, and then only if the amount paid is more than the custodial parent spent on support for the child. If there is a written order or agreement, then the noncustodial parent **can** claim the exemption whenever more than $599 has been paid as support.

Be sure to get and read the tax information pamphlet described in Chapter A12h.

CHAPTER
E

MARITAL SETTLEMENT AGREEMENTS

A Summary Dissolution **requires** a written agreement whenever there is **any** community property and/or bills. A Regular Dissolution does not require a written agreement, but if you and your spouse can communicate, there are many impressive advantages to making a written agreement before the time for the hearing which you should consider (see Chapter A5).

You should remember that a judge is not legally bound by your agreement on matters of child support or child custody and that court orders on such subjects can always be modified in the future in the event of changed circumstances. A spousal support order can also be modified, unless your agreement specifically states that it cannot. In uncontested cases, judges will nearly always follow the agreement of the parties, assuming the agreement falls within the broad range of fairness.

In a Regular Dissolution there are two different ways to proceed with a written agreement: **a)** the relatively simple Agreed Interlocutory Judgment; and **b)** the more detailed and complete Marital Settlement Contract.

E1 | *The Agreed Interlocutory Judgment*

By this method you prepare, well ahead of time, a copy of the Interlocutory Judgment which you intend to take into court, and both parties sign their approval of it. This is an excellent and simple method, with the one disadvantage that many counties treat the Respondent's signature as an appearance and charge you the $70 response fee when you file it. Ask the Clerk's Office if they charge for a consent decree in your county.

Here's how you do it. Read the rest of this book until you understand when the Interlocutory Judgment (Chapter 13) is used and how it is prepared. Then prepare an Interlocutory Judgment which is agreeable to you and your spouse. Between the last order and the line the judge signs, insert the following:

I approve of and consent to the above Judgment.

Dated: _____
                                    Respondent

I consent to the above Judgment and agree to present it to the Court at the time of the hearing.

Dated: _____
                                    Petitioner

Both parties date and sign it. You will need the original and two copies to take to court, and a signed copy for Respondent to keep. Follow all the other instructions in this book, and when you get to the hearing, present the original and two copies to the court. After the hearing give Respondent a court-stamped copy to show that the agreement was completed. When you use this method, you check box 4c or d on the Petition and proceed as if property is being divided by the court.

E2 The Marital Settlement Contract

This kind of agreement is detailed and formal, and a bit more trouble than the first method shown. The response fee of $70 will **not** be charged because of filing this document as of January 1, 1982.

A standard marital settlement agreement is included here so that you can see what one looks like. You can use it as a guide in preparing your own agreement. Use parts that apply to you and disregard the others. Paragraphs X - XIII should **not** be omitted.

If you have any trouble at all understanding the contract, or wording it to fit your own circumstances, do not attempt to do your own. Don't try to do your own if you have a big, intricate estate. If you want to have a contract anyway, get help (see A12). Perhaps you can find an attorney who will prepare a contract for you, then you can do the rest yourself.

Many aspects of any marital settlement agreement can have tax consequences. Be sure to review Tax Information Publication #504 (see Chapter A12). Depending upon what property you have, you may save a lot of money by seeing a tax expert before making this agreement.

You will need an original, a copy for Respondent, and three other copies. Attach the original contract to the original Interlocutory Judgment and a copy of the contract to each copy of the Interlocutory judgment. Take these to court at the time of the hearing. Sacramento County wants a copy of the marital contract attached to the Petition if it is completed at that time.

MARITAL SETTLEMENT AGREEMENT

I, _____, Husband, and I, _____, Wife, agree as follows:

I. GENERALLY: We are now husband and wife. We were married on _____, 19_, and separated on _____, 19_. We make this agreement with reference to the following facts:
  A. Children: There are
    a. no children
    b. the following minor children of the parties (list by full name and give birth date of each).
  B. Unhappy and irreconcilable differences have arisen between us which have caused the irremediable breakdown of our marriage. We now desire and agree to completely settle all of our mutual rights and duties by this agreement.

II. SEPARATION: We agree to live separately and apart, and, except for the duties and obligations imposed and assumed under this agreement, each shall be free from interference and control of the other as fully as if he or she were single. We each agree not to molest, interfere with, or harass the other.

III. CUSTODY OF CHILDREN:

    a. The Wife

    b. The Husband

    c. Husband and Wife, jointly

    d. _____ (other)

shall have the care, custody and control of the minor child(ren) of the parties, subject to the right of the other spouse to visit said child(ren)

    a. at reasonable times and places

    b. as follows: _____

IV. SUPPORT OF CHILDREN: Subject to the power of the court to modify the same, _____ shall pay to _____, as and for child support, the sum of $____ per month per child, a total of $____ per month, payable on the ___ day of each month, beginning on the ___ day of _____, 19_, and continuing for each child until said child dies, marries, becomes self-supporting, or reaches the age of _____, whichever occurs first.

Optional: In addition, during the term of the support obligation for each child, _____ shall

    a. carry and maintain medical and hospital insurance for the benefit of said child;

    b. pay for said child's required/extraordinary medical and dental expenses (to the extent of his ability to do so).

    c. carry and maintain a policy of life insurance in the amount of $_____, and shall name as beneficiaries (Wife/ Husband/ said minor children).

V. PAYMENTS TO SPOUSE: (use A or B)

A. Waiver of Right to Support: In consideration of the other terms of this agreement, both parties waive all right or claim which they may now or may at any future time have to receive support or maintenance from the other. (See Chapter D regarding effect of waiver.)

B. In consideration of the other terms of this marital settlement agreement, _____ agrees to pay _____ the sum of $____ per month, payable on the _ day of each month, beginning _____, 19__, and continuing until (some certain date/ the death of either party/ remarriage of the recipient/ some precise condition) whichever shall occur first. The parties intend that this amount (may/may not) be modified by court action in the future. (**Note:** no amount of cohabitation will equal remarriage, so be very clear if you intend some amount of cohabitation to be a condition to terminate spousal support.)

VI. PROPERTY TRANSFERRED TO WIFE: Husband transfers and quitclaims to Wife all his right, title, and interest in the following items: (list and **indicate value** of each item. Give legal description of any real estate).

VII. PROPERTY TRANSFERRED TO HUSBAND: Wife transfers and quitclaims to Husband all her right, title, and interest in the following items: (list and **indicate value** of each item. Give legal description of any real estate).

Note about Pension Plans: If there is a community interest in a pension plan, be sure to deal with it clearly in this agreement. If it is to be given entirely to the employee spouse, list it in item VI or VII. If there is to be a waiver, put it in here, using the language suggested in Chapter B3c as your guide. If the matter is to be reserved for the future, put that in here like this: VIII. PENSION PLAN. The parties intend that the community interest in the pension plan of (Husband/Wife), (full identification of plan), will be valued and divided when the employee-spouse first becomes eligible to receive payments under said plan. To this end, the parties agree to keep each other notified of changes in address and of any changes in pension plan provisions. (Employee spouse) specifically agrees not to apply for or accept benefits under said plan without prior written notice to (other spouse) and application to a court for determination and division of community property rights in said plan.

Note about separate property: If there is separate property or obligations that you want clearly confirmed as such, put that in like this: VIII. SEPARATE PROPERTY. The parties agree that the assets and obligations listed below are the separate property of (Husband/Wife) and are hereby confirmed as such: (list).

Alternative Method to Divide Property
(for cases with little or no significant property)

Husband and Wife agree that they have already divided their property to their mutual satisfaction, and each hereby transfers and quitclaims to the other any and all interest in any property in the possession of the other, and agrees that whatever property the other may possess is now the sole and separate property of the other.

VIII. DEBTS:

Husband shall pay the following debts, and indemnify and hold Wife harmless therefrom: (list).

Wife shall pay the following debts, and indemnify and hold Husband harmless therefrom: (list).

Husband and Wife each promise the other that they shall not incur any debt or obligation for which the other may be liable, and each agrees that if any claim be brought seeking to hold one liable for the subsequent debts of the other, or for any act or omission of the other, then each will hold the other harmless, and defend such claim.

IX. TAXES:

A. Any tax refunds for the current fiscal year shall be distributed as follows: (specify).

B. Any deficiencies for the current year shall be paid as follows: (specify).

C. (Husband/Wife) may claim the tax exemption for (name of children). Optional: ...for any year in which support payments for said child are not over two months in arrears.

X. EXECUTION OF INSTRUMENTS: Each agrees to execute and deliver any documents, make all endorsements, and do all acts which are necessary or convenient to carry out the terms of this agreement.

XI. PRESENTATION TO COURT: This agreement shall be presented to the court for incorporation and merger into the Interlocutory Judgment in any dissolution proceeding between the parties.

XII. DISCLOSURES: Each party has made a full and honest disclosure to the other of all current finances and assets, and each enters into this agreement in reliance thereon.

XIII. BINDING EFFECT: This agreement, and each provision thereof, is expressly made binding upon the heirs, assigns, executors, administrators, representatives, and successors in interest of each party.

Dated: _____
                                        Husband

Dated: _____
                                        Wife

F

Regular or Summary Dissolution
WHICH IS FOR YOU?

In 1979, California lawmakers gave us a second way to get a divorce. The way it has always been done is still exactly the same, and is now called **Regular Dissolution.** The brand new and much simpler procedure is called **Summary Dissolution.** This book tells you how to choose and how to handle either procedure for yourself.

Not everyone is eligible for the Summary Dissolution, and of those who are eligible, not everyone will want to use it. The Regular method has advantages even for those who are qualified to use the Summary method.

The Summary Dissolution is a greatly simplified divorce procedure that requires only two easy forms, and there is no court appearance. In order to use it, you and your spouse must **both** sign a Petition form and you **must** prepare and sign a property agreement. These papers **must** be filed before your fifth wedding anniversary. When you sign the Petition, you and your spouse are taking an oath by which you swear that:

1. Both spouses have read and understood the Summary Dissolution Booklet (free from your County Clerk's Office);

2. One spouse has lived in California for at least six months and in the county of filing for at least three months immediately before the date you file your Petition;

3. There are no minor children and the wife is not pregnant;

4. Neither spouse has **any** interest in **any** real estate **anywhere**;

5. There is less than $4,000 in community debts, not counting car loans;

6. There is less than $12,000 in community property, not counting cars; and,

7. Neither spouse owns over $12,000 separately, not counting cars.

In addition, both spouses must give up all rights to spousal support. If there is absolutely no property and no debts, the property agreement can be omitted.

If you can meet these requirements **and** if the papers can be prepared and filed before your fifth wedding anniversary, then you can use the summary

---

procedure. After you file your Petition, there follows a six month waiting period, after which either spouse may file a simple form requesting that the divorce be granted. Unless and until the final judgment has been requested, granted and entered in the clerk's records, there is **no** divorce.

Revocation: At any time before the final is requested, **either** spouse may file a simple form revoking the whole proceeding, killing it. Dead. If this happens, either spouse can still file a Regular Dissolution.

Comments

The idea of a law designed for use directly by people is very good, but this one is limited in scope and too risky for most people to use.

The worst problem is the fact that either spouse can revoke the proceeding at any time before the final judgment is entered. Therefore, for **at least** six months, maybe more, your dissolution is at risk. Divorce often involves personal dramas and emotional turmoil. It is a time when otherwise reasonable people can play bad games. Are you absolutely certain that your spouse won't spoil the Summary Dissolution for the next six months or so?

The five year deadline seems unnecessary if all the other qualifications are met. Because of it, a couple may be inclined to rush things if their deadline is near, just to get the papers in on time. This would be a big mistake.

Advice

Even if you **are** eligible for the Summary Dissolution procedure, you should **only** do it if you can start in plenty of time to make important decisions, get the property agreement worked out, and the papers filed without feeling under pressure to meet the deadline. This is too important to rush, and mistakes may come back to haunt you later.

You should **not** do a Summary Dissolution unless you can be certain that your agreements with your spouse are firm and mutual. If there is even a small chance that during the next six or more months one spouse might become temperamental, uncertain, or unstable enough to revoke the dissolution, then you would both be better off filing a Regular Dissolution to begin with.

The Regular Dissolution is really not so hard. It is a bit more trouble in that you have to file a fistful of forms, and probably you will make one brief court appearance, but it is also a lot more stable and certain. It is more difficult to frustrate and gets harder to disrupt with each step. It costs about the same. Take a look at Chapter 3 in Part Two to see exactly what is involved in doing a Regular Dissolution.

If you do **not** meet the qualifications for the Summary Dissolution, your choice is made for you - you must use the Regular Dissolution procedure. If you **do** meet them, then read Part One of this book and look over Part Two to become familiar with the Regular Dissolution. Consider our comments and advice and then choose which procedure you want to use.

PART TWO: HOW TO DO YOUR OWN REGULAR DISSOLUTION

HOW TO USE THE FORMS

Part Two tells you exactly how to do your own **Regular** Dissolution. Chapter F, above, describes the Regular and Summary Dissolution procedures and tells you how to choose which one to use.

All dissolutions in California, whether prepared by you or by an attorney, must be filed on standard forms designed by the California Judicial Council. A complete set of these forms is in the back of this book. Forms are also available at your County Clerk's Office where you should be able to get a set for free or for a minimal charge, but occasionally they can be less than helpful. If you want to order a complete set, send $6 to Nolo Press, Box 544, Occidental, CA. 95465.

In the chapters which follow, there are instructions on how to complete each form, together with an explanation and detailed illustrations. Some forms may not be necessary in your case. Just use the ones that you need. Keep your papers safe, neat, organized, and all together in one place.

Here are some general instructions which apply to all of the forms:

1a *Use a Typewriter*

The forms should be completed carefully and exactly as shown, with a typewriter. It would be best to use the larger size type (Pica), as at least one county, San Diego, has refused to accept forms with smaller type (Elite).

1b *Captions*

At the top of each form is a heading, called a caption, which is filled out like this:

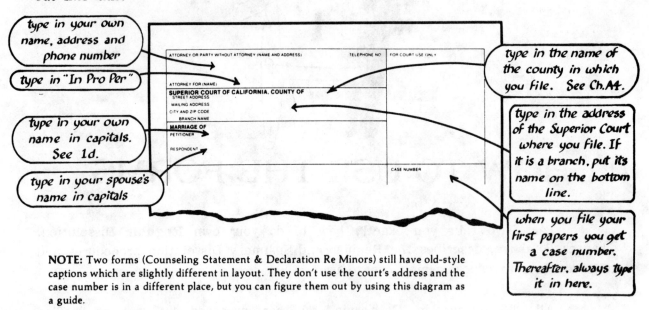

> type in your own name, address and phone number

> type in "In Pro Per"

> type in your own name in capitals. See 1d.

> type in your spouse's name in capitals

> type in the name of the county in which you file. See Ch.A4.

> type in the address of the Superior Court where you file. If it is a branch, put its name on the bottom line.

> when you file your first papers you get a case number. Thereafter, always type it in here.

NOTE: Two forms (Counseling Statement & Declaration Re Minors) still have old-style captions which are slightly different in layout. They don't use the court's address and the case number is in a different place, but you can figure them out by using this diagram as a guide.

1c *Petitioner/Respondent/In pro per*

The Petitioner is the spouse that files the papers and goes to court. The Respondent is the other spouse. Apart from possibly signing a Waiver, Acknowlegment form, or Marital Agreement, the Respondent does nothing - files no papers, does not go to court. The words "in pro per" appear in the caption and at other places. This is abbreviated legal Latin, meaning that you are appearing for yourself, without an attorney.

1d *Names*

Although not required, it is a good idea to use full names in these papers. Be consistent - names should appear exactly the same way each time, including signatures. The court will not know, for instance, that John Smith, J.W. Smith, John W. Smith and J. Wilson Smith are different names for the same person. It is good form to type in the names in capitals. Use the names in normal order - last names go last. Use the wife's married name, unless the form asks for her maiden name.

1e Number of Copies

The court always gets the original of each form, the Respondent gets a copy, and you keep a copy for your own files. That means you will need the original and two copies, but make one extra copy of each form just in case. At least one County Clerk (Contra Costa) asks for an extra copy of each form when you file your papers in a branch office.

Type each form neatly, check for errors, then have the desired number of copies made on a Xerox or similar photo copy machine. To find copy machines in your area, check the yellow pages of your phone book under "copying and duplicating service," or ask at the public library or the County Clerk's Office. When you copy a form which has material on the back, you will end up with two pages - staple them together at the top left hand corner.

1f Oaths

At some places in these forms you will place your signature on what is called a "declaration under penalty of perjury." It looks like this:

I declare under penalty of perjury that the foregoing is true and correct and that this declaration is executed on (date): Date at (place): City or location where you sign , California.

Your name *your signature*
(Type or print name) (Signature of declarant)

This has the same effect as an oath or sworn statement. The word "executed" means "signed." To fill it in, type in your name, the date signed, the city or location in California where you sign it and add your signature.

If you are not inside the state of California when you sign the oath, you will have to change the first lines to look like this:

under the laws of the State of California
I declare under penalty of perjury/that the foregoing is true and correct and that this declaration is executed on (date): Date at (place): City or location where you sign California.

Your name *your signature*
(Type or print name) (Signature of declarant)

HOW TO FILE YOUR PAPERS

Filing papers is easy. All you do is take them down to the County Clerk's Office and hand them to the clerk. When you file the Petition you must also pay the filing fee.

The county in which you file is determined by the residency requirement (Chapter A8) and is most often the one you live in. Before you go there, call the Clerk's Office and ask questions such as how to find their office, the proper place to file your papers, whether there is a branch court any nearer to you, if there is a conciliation court in your county, how much the filing fees are for a dissolution case, and so on.

When you file your first papers, the clerk will give you a case number. From this time on, **all** documents filed in your case **must** have this number on them.

Business with the Clerk's Office can be done by mail or in person. Filing in person is preferred, if it is not too inconvenient. When you file a form, include all the copies with the original so they can stamp the copies. When you file by mail, be sure to send along a self-addressed, stamped envelope for the return of your copies.

The clerks will not be willing to give you legal advice because they are not attorneys, and it would be illegal for them to do so. But if they wish to they can help you a lot with information about the filing of papers and how matters are handled in their county. Don't be afraid to ask questions. Stay polite no matter how they act.

FILING FEES: This fee is paid when you file the first papers. It has gone up sharply, and is now about $90 in most counties. Some counties get more by imposing extra fees for setting your case for the hearing or giving out your final decree. This is one thing you can ask about when you first contact the Clerk's Office. Fees should be paid with cash or money order as they probably will not take a personal check. If you are too poor to pay the Petitioner's filing fee, you can submit the Pauper's Oath described in Appendix B and possibly you can get the fees waived.

There is also a filing fee of about $70 for the Response which you should not have to pay, since Respondent is not filing any papers. However, some counties are getting quite greedy these days and will use almost any excuse to get the extra fee, so if you file anything with Respondent's signature on it other than the Acknowledgment, the Military Waiver, and the Marital Settlement Agreement, then be prepared to pay. Practices vary, so ask your County Clerk.

CHECK LIST

This your guide to the "how to do it" section -- a step-by-step check list showing you what to do, when to do it, and referring you to other chapters to find out more about each step.

Step 1: File the First Papers

Prepare and file the following with the County Clerk (see Chapter 2):
SUMMONS (Chapter 5)
PETITION (Chapter 6. Attach the Declaration Re Minors if it is required - see Chapter 6, note 3)
CONFIDENTIAL STATEMENT (if required - see Chapter 7)
The filing fee: money order or cash (Chapter 2), or file the Pauper's Oath (Appendix B)
(A few counties use a special local form when filing in a branch office - see Chapter 4)

Step 2: Serve Papers On Your Spouse

See Chapter 8. Have the following items served on Respondent:
One **copy** of the **SUMMONS**
One **copy** of the **PETITION** (and Declaration Re Minors if there are children)
One **blank COUNSELING STATEMENT** (if required - Chapter 7)

Step 3: File the Second Papers

Wait at least 30 days after the effective date of service of papers on your spouse, then file the following:

PROOF OF SERVICE (on back of **original** SUMMONS) (Chapter 9)

REQUEST FOR ENTRY OF DEFAULT (Chapter 10)

FINANCIAL DECLARATION (Chapter 11)

(Several counties require you to perform Step 4 with a local form a this time. See Chapter 12, ask the Clerk's Office)

(Local rules - some counties want the Interlocutory Judgment and Notice of Entry at this time - ask the Clerk's Office)

Step 4: Get a Date for the Hearing

See Chapter 12a. A few counties use a local form to set the hearing - ask the Clerk's Office if one is required in your county.

Step 5: The Hearing

See Chapter 12. If you have not already filed them, prepare the following forms and take them with you:

INTERLOCUTORY JUDGMENT (Chapter 13)

NOTICE OF ENTRY OF JUDGMENT (Chapter 14)

Step 6: Request the Final Judgment

Wait at least 6 months after the effective date of service of process upon your spouse (see Chapter 8), and at least 2 months after entry of the Interlocutory Judgment (see Chapter 14), then prepare and file:

REQUEST FOR FINAL JUDGMENT (Chapter 15)

FINAL JUDGMENT (Chapter 16)

NOTICE OF ENTRY OF JUDGMENT (Chapter 14)

(Many counties require a $2 fee at this time - cash or M.O.)

When the Final Judgment is entered, you are finished.

LOCAL FORMS

Dissolution forms were standardized by the state in 1970 in order to make law practice more uniform and efficient. This was a very good idea, but since that time many different counties have frustrated the goal by requiring various local forms in addition the official set. We include and discuss them in this book, but we can't always keep track of them all, so if you come across a form you can't figure out by reading these pages, just mail two blank copies of it to **Nolo Press** with a stamped self-addressed envelope and we will send you instructions.

Call your County Clerk's Office, Civil Division, and ask what special local forms they use in an uncontested dissolution proceeding, and get copies of them. Ask at what point they are to be filed.

The first time you might run into a local form is when you file your first papers. If your county has branch courts, and if you want to file in a branch instead of the main office, then they may require a Certificate or Declaration of Assignment. We show two of them here for your information, but please note that forms from other counties may be slightly different. What they all basically want to know is what court district you are filing in (get the correct name from the Clerk's office) and the reason why - which is invariably because you or Respondent have residence in that district - so if asked, then put down "(Petitioner/Respondent) resides in said district at (give address)."

The second time you are likely to meet a local form is at the filing of the second papers, when you request a hearing. These are illustrated at the end of Chapter 12, where they are most relevant.

Figure 1: CERTIFICATE OF ASSIGNMENT
(Los Angeles County)

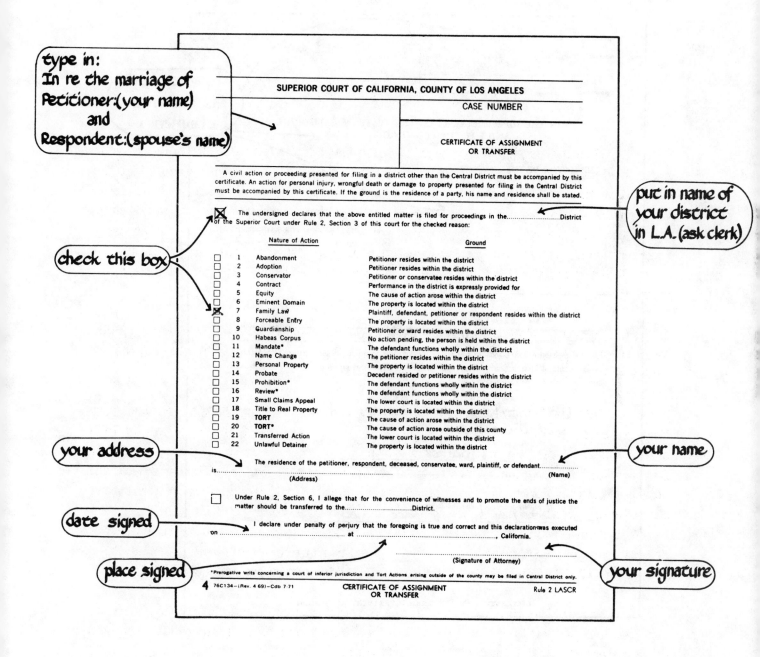

type in:
In re the marriage of
Petitioner:(your name)
and
Respondent:(spouse's name)

check this box

your address

date signed

place signed

put in name of your district in L.A. (ask clerk)

your name

your signature

SUPERIOR COURT OF CALIFORNIA, COUNTY OF LOS ANGELES

CASE NUMBER

CERTIFICATE OF ASSIGNMENT
OR TRANSFER

A civil action or proceeding presented for filing in a district other than the Central District must be accompanied by this certificate. An action for personal injury, wrongful death or damage to property presented for filing in the Central District must be accompanied by this certificate. If the ground is the residence of a party, his name and residence shall be stated.

☒ The undersigned declares that the above entitled matter is filed for proceedings in the.........................District of the Superior Court under Rule 2, Section 3 of this court for the checked reason:

	Nature of Action	Ground
1	Abandonment	Petitioner resides within the district
2	Adoption	Petitioner resides within the district
3	Conservator	Petitioner or conservatee resides within the district
4	Contract	Performance in the district is expressly provided for
5	Equity	The cause of action arose within the district
6	Eminent Domain	The property is located within the district
7	Family Law	Plaintiff, defendant, petitioner or respondent resides within the district
8	Forceable Entry	The property is located within the district
9	Guardianship	Petitioner or ward resides within the district
10	Habeas Corpus	No action pending, the person is held within the district
11	Mandate*	The defendant functions wholly within the district
12	Name Change	The petitioner resides within the district
13	Personal Property	The property is located within the district
14	Probate	Decedent resided or petitioner resides within the district
15	Prohibition*	The defendant functions wholly within the district
16	Review*	The defendant functions wholly within the district
17	Small Claims Appeal	The lower court is located within the district
18	Title to Real Property	The property is located within the district
19	TORT	The cause of action arose within the district
20	TORT*	The cause of action arose outside of this county
21	Transferred Action	The lower court is located within the district
22	Unlawful Detainer	The property is located within the district

The residence of the petitioner, respondent, deceased, conservatee, ward, plaintiff, or defendant..........................
is.......................................
(Address)
(Name)

☐ Under Rule 2, Section 6, I allege that for the convenience of witnesses and to promote the ends of justice the matter should be transferred to the.........................District.

I declare under penalty of perjury that the foregoing is true and correct and this declaration was executed on .... at ...., California.

....
(Signature of Attorney)

*Prerogative writs concerning a court of inferior jurisdiction and Tort Actions arising outside of the county may be filed in Central District only.

4 76C134—(Rev. 4 69)—Cdb 7-71   CERTIFICATE OF ASSIGNMENT   Rule 2 LASCR
OR TRANSFER

Figure 1a: # DECLARATION FOR ASSIGNMENT
(San Mateo County)

Attorney(s) for_____

Address_____

_____

Telephone_____

type caption as shown in chapter 1

IN THE SUPERIOR COURT OF THE STATE OF CALIFORNIA
IN AND FOR THE COUNTY OF

IN THE MATTER OF THE   **MARRIAGE**
OF

NO. *type case #*

DECLARATION FOR ASSIGNMENT
TO NORTHERN DEPARTMENT

I, _____*Your name*_____, hereby declare:
That I am the attorney for the___*Petitioner, in pro per*_____
in the above-entitled matter, and that said matter may properly be assigned to the Northern Department of
the above-entitled Superior Court at South San Francisco, California, as provided in the Rules of the said
Superior Court, for the following reason:

(Petitioner/Respondent) resides within
said district at:

(address)
_____

I declare under penalty of perjury that the foregoing is true and correct.
Executed on___*date signed*_____, at ___*place signed*_____, California

Signature
_____
Attorney for ___*Petitioner, in pro per*

DECLARATION FOR NORTHERN DEPARTMENT ASSIGNMENT

THE SUMMONS

WHAT IT IS

The Summons is a message from the court to the Respondent. It states that a Petition has been filed which concerns the Respondent, and that if there is no written Response within 30 days the court may go ahead and grant the Petitioner what has been asked for. A copy of the Summons has to be served on Respondent along with the Petition (see Chapter 8).

On the back of the Summons is another form, the Proof of Service (Chapter 9). When you file your first papers (Step 1) the clerk will put a seal on the original Summons and return it to you with the copies. Make sure that you keep track of the **original** Summons, because you **must** file it when you file the Proof of Service.

HOW TO FILL IT OUT

Fill out the Summons as shown in Fig. 2. Prepare the original and make 3 copies (see 1e).

Note: If you lose or misplace your original Summons, you are in for a little extra trouble because you will have to prepare and file a Declaration of Service of Lost Summons. If this misfortune happens to you, send $3 to **Nolo Press** for forms and instructions. Ask for the Lost Summons set.

Figure 2: HOW TO FILL OUT THE SUMMONS

(handwritten note, left) type caption as shown in chapter 1

ATTORNEY OR PARTY WITHOUT ATTORNEY (NAME AND ADDRESS):	TELEPHONE NO.:	FOR COURT USE ONLY

ATTORNEY FOR (NAME):

SUPERIOR COURT OF CALIFORNIA, COUNTY OF
STREET ADDRESS:
MAILING ADDRESS:
CITY AND ZIP CODE:
BRANCH NAME:

MARRIAGE OF
PETITIONER:

RESPONDENT:

SUMMONS (FAMILY LAW)	CASE NUMBER:

NOTICE!

You have been sued. The court may decide against you without your being heard unless you respond within 30 days. Read the information below.

If you wish to seek the advice of an attorney in this matter, you should do so promptly so that your response or pleading, if any, may be filed on time.

¡AVISO!

Usted ha sido demandado. El tribunal puede decidir contra Ud. sin audiencia a menos que Ud. responda dentro de 30 días. Lea la información que sigue.

Si Usted desea solicitar el consejo de un abogado en este asunto, debería hacerlo inmediatamente, de esta manera, su respuesta o alegación, si hay alguna, puede ser registrada a tiempo.

1. TO THE RESPONDENT

The petitioner has filed a petition concerning your marriage. If you fail to file a response within 30 days of the date that this summons is served on you, your default may be entered and the court may enter a judgment containing injunctive or other orders concerning division of property, spousal support, child custody, child support, attorney fees, costs, and such other relief as may be granted by the court. The garnishment of wages, taking of money or property, or other court authorized proceedings may also result.

Dated: . . . .   Clerk, By _____ , Deputy

(SEAL)

2. NOTICE TO THE PERSON SERVED. You are served
   a. ☐ As an individual
   b. ☐ On behalf of Respondent

   Under:
   ☐ CCP 416.60 (Minor)
   ☐ CCP 416.70 (Ward or Conservatee)
   ☐ CCP 416.90 (Individual)
   ☐ Other (specify):

   c. ☐ By personal delivery on (Date):

(See reverse for Proof of Service)

(handwritten note, right) Check box 2a. After service, if Respondent was served personally (see Ch.8d), also check box 2c and type in date of delivery.

The response (printed form rule 1282) and other permitted papers must be in the form prescribed by the California Rules of Court. They must be filed in this court with the proper filing fee and proof of service of a copy of each on petitioner. The time when the 30 days to respond begins may vary depending on the method of service. For example, see CCP 413.10-415.50.

Form Adopted by Rule 1283
Judicial Council of California
Revised Effective January 1, 1980

**SUMMONS
(FAMILY LAW)**

CC 4503
CCP 412.20
CRC 1216

THE PETITION

WHAT IT IS

The Petition states basic information about your marriage and tells the court what you want done. When it is served on the Respondent (Step 2) it gives notice of what's happening in court. If Respondent sees the Petition and declines to respond, then the judge is free to assume that Respondent has no objection to the facts and claims stated in it.

HOW TO FILL IT OUT

Fill out the Petition as shown in Figs. 3 and 4. Prepare the original and make 3 copies (see 1e).

NOTES FOR THE FRONT OF THE PETITION

Note 1: The date of your separation is the last day you were living together under the same roof. Sometimes it happens, say for economic reasons, that couples continue to live together under the same roof but still want to dissolve their marriage. In such a case, separation comes when the couple stops sleeping together **and** also stops thinking of themselves as living together as man and wife. If you don't know the exact date, don't worry, just get as close as you can. If you have separated several times, use the most recent date.

Note 2: The number of children you have should include only **minor** children born to or adopted by both you and your spouse. Don't include stepchildren who have not been adopted by the stepparent. If the wife is pregnant, include the unborn child and in the space provided for the name of child, put "one unborn."

Note 3: If there are minor children then read over Item 3(c)(1) on the Petition very carefully to see if you can swear to it. If you can, then check the boxes and fill in the address of Petitioner or Respondent (or both where the

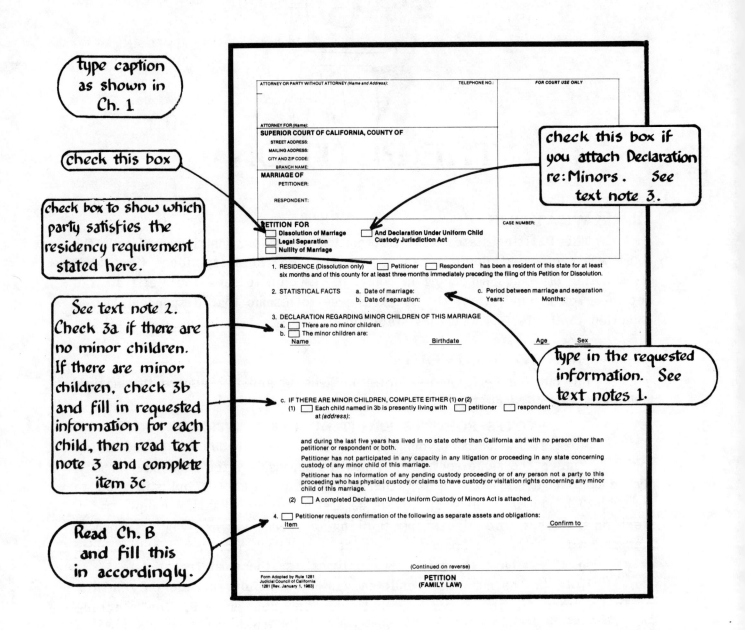

(continued from preceding page)

children reside in both places). If the printed statement is not accurate for your case, then check box 3(c)(2), fill out the Declaration Re Minors form as shown in Figs. 5 and 6 and attach it to the Petition.

Note 4: If you need more space to complete any item, type in "See Petition Continuation Page A." Type that heading on a sheet of 8 1/2 x 11 paper, then for each item continued you type a paragraph heading "Continuation of Petition Item (number of item being continued) , and complete your list. Staple the original and copies to original and copies of the Petition.

Note 5: Read Chapter B very carefully. The way the court will relate to your property depends upon how you fill out the Petition. Items 4 and 5 in the Petition are where you tell the court about your property ("property" includes both assets and obligations). Your options are explained below.

ITEM 4. CONFIRMATION OF SEPARATE ASSETS AND OBLIGATIONS:

If you want certain property to be confirmed as the separate asset or debt of either you or your spouse, then list it here and indicate to whom (Petitioner or Respondent) it is to be confirmed. Be sure to include any pension plan that you had entirely and only after separation.

NOTES FOR THE BACK OF THE PETITION

ITEM 5. DECLARATION REGARDING...ASSETS AND OBLIGATIONS:

a.   There are no such assets or obligations subject to disposition by the court in this proceeding.

When you check this box, the court will not inquire much into your property nor make orders about it. Check this box when there is no property, or when the property has already been divided up, or if for some other reason you don't need a court order, such as when your spouse is long gone, doesn't care or has abandoned the property to you. Do **not** check this box if there is or may ever be any disagreement between you about some item of property, or where there is any real estate which has not already been divided legally, or if there is a community interest in a pension plan (see Chapter B3c).

b.   All such assets and obligations have been disposed of by written agreement.

If you check the second box, you are telling the court that you and your spouse have made a written agreement about your property (see Chapter E). At the

---

THE PETITION 73

Figure 4: HOW TO FILL OUT THE PETITION
(back)

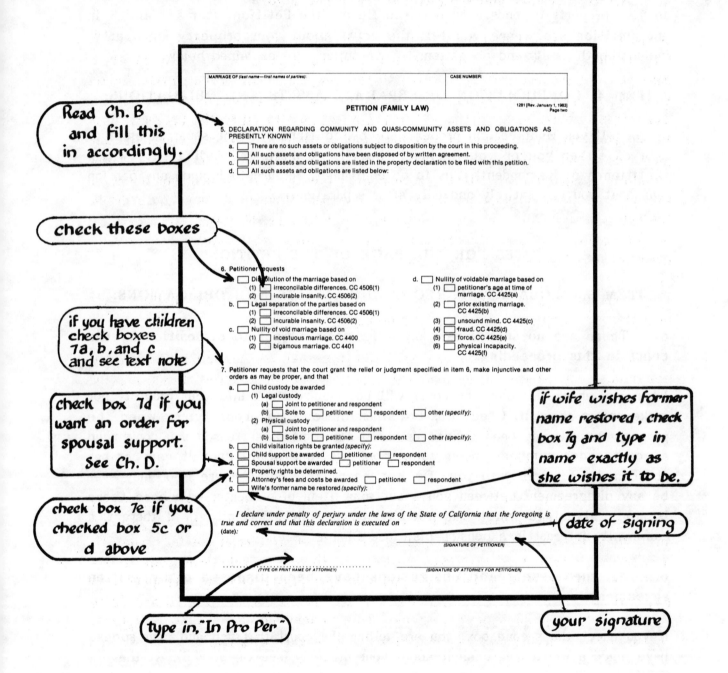

Read Ch. B and fill this in accordingly.

check these boxes

if you have children check boxes 7a, b, and c and see text note

check box 7d if you want an order for spousal support. See Ch. D.

check box 7e if you checked box 5c or d above

type in, "In Pro Per"

if wife wishes former name restored, check box 7g and type in name exactly as she wishes it to be.

date of signing

your signature

---

hearing, the court will examine the agreement and will almost certainly approve its execution and terms.

c.   All such assets and obligations are listed in the property declaration to be filed with this petition.
d.   All such assets and obligations are listed below.

Boxes c and d have the same effect, the only difference being that you check box c when your list is too long to put on the face of the Petition, in which case you use the Property Declaration form (see Ch. 11 for instructions). Unless your list is very small indeed, it is better to use this form. Even if you list everything on the face of the Petition, you should still study the property form to see how the items should be grouped and presented, and as a check list for your assets and debts. Major items should be individually listed: cars, bank accounts, pension plans, stocks, accumulated vacation pay, trusts, and things of special importance to you. Real estate can be identified by its common address. It's not necessary, but to cover property that you might have forgotten, or might discover later, you can put, "and any other community property of description and value unknown at this time."

You **must** fill in your best estimate of the fair market value for all items, and indicate your proposed division of the property.

If you check either box, you can still put together an Agreed Interlocutory Judgment or a Written Agreement with your spouse (see Chapter E) and present it at the hearing.

ITEM 7: IF YOU HAVE MINOR CHILDREN

Note for 7a-c: Read Chapter C2. Pure joint custody is requested by checking a(1)(a) and a(2)(a) to ask for both legal and physical joint custody. In that case visitation is not requested, and child support need not be requested. You can also request joint legal custody, with sole physical custody to one party, or you can request sole legal and sole physical custody for one party. In any but the first case (pure joint custody) you should check boxes 7b and 7c to request visitation and support orders. When checking 7b be sure to type in "Petitioner" or "Respondent" to indicate who is to get visitation.

Figure 5: HOW TO FILL OUT
THE DECLARATION RE: MINORS
(front)

type caption as shown in Ch. 1

name, place of birth, birthdate, and sex of first child.

child's present address and time living there. Give name, address and relationship of custodian.

child's addresses and custodian for past five years.

Give same info for second child...Add extra sheets with same info for any other minors.

number of *minor* children of marriage at time of filing.

number of extra pages attached, if any.

Name, Address and Telephone of Attorney(s)

Space Below Use of Court Clerk Only

Attorney(s) for

SUPERIOR COURT OF CALIFORNIA, COUNTY OF

In re the marriage of

Petitioner

and

Respondent

CASE NUMBER

DECLARATION UNDER UNIFORM CUSTODY OF MINORS ACT

1 The number of minor children subject to this proceeding is _____ The name, place of birth, birthdate and sex of each child, the present address, periods of residence and places where each child has lived within the past five (5) years, and the name, present address and relationship to the child of each person with whom the child has lived during that time are: (See footnote *)

Child's Name A		Place of Birth	Birthdate	Sex
Period of Residence	Address	Person Child Lived With (Name and Present Address)		Relationship
to present				
to				
to				
to				

Child's Name B		Place of Birth	Birthdate	Sex
Period of Residence	Address	Person Child Lived With (Name and Present Address)		Relationship
to present				
to				
to				
to				
to				

Total Number of Continuation Pages Attached _____

Singular includes plural. Declaration under penalty of perjury must be signed in California (CCP 2015.5.) Affidavit is required when signed outside California. When declaration applies to more than two children attach additional page (CRC 201 (b))

Form Approved by the
Judicial Council of California
Effective January 1, 1975

DECLARATION UNDER UNIFORM CUSTODY OF MINORS ACT

CC 5158

Figure 6: HOW TO FILL OUT THE DECLARATION RE: MINORS

(back)

check first box if there have been no custody proceedings anywhere re: the minor child(ren).

otherwise check the appropriate second box and fill in the requested info.

check first box if no person (other than you & spouse) claims custody or visiting rights.

otherwise check second box & give requested info.

date of signing

type your name

place of signing

your signature

2. ☐ I have not participated as a party, witness, or in any other capacity in any other litigation or custody proceeding, in this or any other state, concerning custody of a child subject to this proceeding.

☐ I have participated as a party, witness, or in some other capacity in other litigation or custody proceeding, in this or some other state, concerning custody of a child subject to this proceeding, as follows:

   a. Name of each child:

   b. Capacity of declarant:

   c. Court and state:

   d. Date of court order or judgment (if any):

3. ☐ I have no information of any custody proceeding pending in a court of this or any other state concerning a child subject to this proceeding, other than that set out in item 2.

☐ I have the following information concerning a custody proceeding pending in a court of this or some other state concerning a child subject to this proceeding, other than that set out in item 2:

   a. Name of each child:

   b. Nature of proceeding:

   c. Court and state:

   d. Status of proceeding:

4. ☐ I do not know of any person not a party to this proceeding who has physical custody or claims to have custody or visitation rights with respect to any child subject to this proceeding.

☐ I know that the following named person not a party to this proceeding has physical custody or claims custody or visitation rights with respect to a child subject to this proceeding:

   a. Name and address of person: b. Name and address of person: c. Name and address of person:

   ☐ Has physical custody   ☐ Has physical custody   ☐ Has physical custody
   ☐ Claims custody rights   ☐ Claims custody rights   ☐ Claims custody rights
   ☐ Claims visitation rights   ☐ Claims visitation rights   ☐ Claims visitation rights

   a. Name of each child: b. Name of each child: c. Name of each child:

I declare under penalty of perjury that the foregoing, including any attachments, is true and correct and that this declaration is executed on (Date) . . . . at (Place) . . . . ,California.

. . . .   _____
(Type or print name)   (Signature of Declarant)

NOTICE TO DECLARANT: You have a continuing duty to inform this court of any information you obtain of any custody proceeding, in this or in any other state, concerning a child subject to this proceeding.

THE PETITION 77

⑦ COUNSELING STATEMENT

About 17 counties have a Conciliation Court, designed to provide counseling for free or cheap to those who wish it. In those counties you **must** file the Confidential Counseling Statement declaring whether or not you wish to talk to a counselor. Maybe they can help save your marriage, but more important, maybe they can help make your dissolution easier and more successful. Maybe not. One visit is free and won't slow down your action. Ask your Clerk whether there is a Conciliation Court in your County, and only file this form if there is one. Before filling it out, make a copy of the **blank** form to serve on Respondent, then prepare an original and two copies to file.

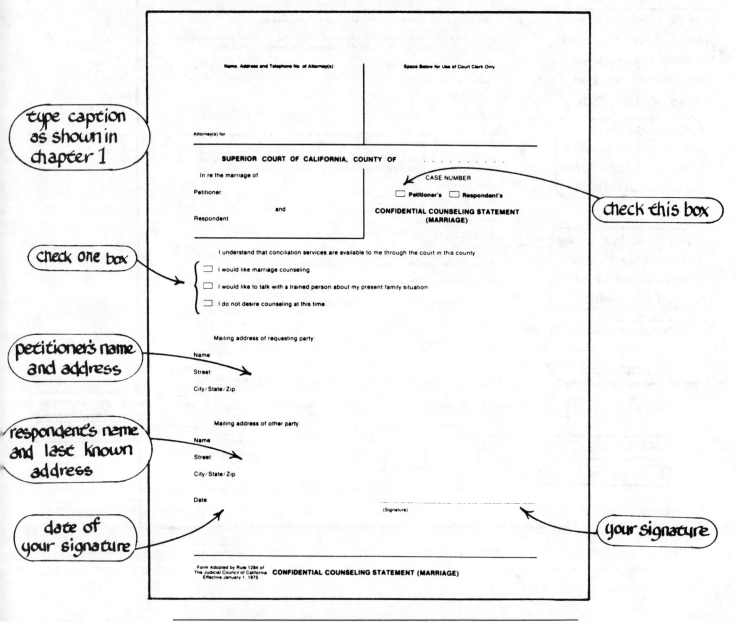

type caption as shown in chapter 1

check this box

check one box

petitioner's name and address

respondent's name and last known address

date of your signature

your signature

HOW TO SERVE PAPERS ON YOUR SPOUSE

When the first papers have been prepared and filed (Step 1) the court does not have power to do anything until notice of the Petition has been formally given to your spouse. The step of formal notice is called "service of process." If Respondent will sign the Waiver (Appendix A), you can avoid this process. It costs about $70 to file, but it is faster and easier.

8a *Who can serve the papers*

The papers must be served by someone who is at least 18 years of age and not a party to the action. This means that you can't do it yourself because you are one of the parties. A relative **may** do it, but it would look better if the person were unrelated. The person who serves the papers for you must also fill out and sign a Proof of Service form (see Chapter 9) to prove to the court that papers were served properly.

8b *The papers to be served*

You must serve your spouse with a **copy** of the Summons (not the original) and a copy of the Petition. In addition, if you filed the papers in a county which has a Conciliation Court, you must also serve a **blank** Counseling Statement (see Chapter 7). These papers need not be filled out or returned.

8c | *Choosing the method of service*

There are several different ways in which papers can be served upon your spouse:

1. Where spouse is located inside California:
   a. Personal service (8d), or
   b. Service by mail and acknowledgment (8e).

2. Where spouse is located outside California:
   a. Either method above (8d or 8e), or
   b. Service by certified or registered mail (8f).

If you can't serve your spouse **inside** California, the court's power to order your spouse to pay support or to do certain acts (i.e., hand over property) may possibly be restricted. It would therefore be better if you can get your spouse to sign the Waiver (Appendix A), which gives the court full jurisdiction.

3. Where spouse cannot be located anywhere:

If you can't find your spouse, the service of process becomes much more difficult. Try very hard to locate him/her. Get the most recent address you can and try serving papers by mail as described in 8e or 8f - maybe they will get through. If nothing works, you can only proceed by Publication of Summons as described in Appendix D.

4. The Waiver - For Cooperative & Military Spouses:

In any case the Appearance and Waiver (Appendix A) has some advantages because it eliminates the need for service of process, 30 days wait, and filing the default. You can use this method with any cooperative spouse, but unless your spouse is in the military and thus exempted, it will cost about $70 for the Response fee when it is filed. If your spouse is on **active** military duty, you cannot use any other method. You **must** use the Waiver, and your spouse must be willing to sign it. This is the **only** way you can proceed on your own if your spouse is in the military.

Look over the various methods and decide which you will use. If your spouse will be cooperative, then service by mail and acknowledgment (8e) will be easiest and cheapest. If your spouse is out of state and will not try to avoid receiving a certified letter, service by certified or registered airmail (8f) is good. If you know where your spouse is located, but aren't sure how much cooperation you will get, then personal service (8d) is most certain. If in doubt, try one of the easier methods first.

8d Personal service

If you know where your spouse can be located, you can have papers served personally. This means that some person (over 18, not you) must personally hand your spouse the papers to be served (8b). The person making service can be a professional process server, or a Sheriff, Marshal, or Constable. If service can be made **inside** California you could have a friend do it for you.

Whoever is going to serve your spouse must be given the following items:

1. A photo or description of your spouse.
2. The best and most complete information about where your spouse can be found, at home and at work.
3. The papers listed in 8b.
4. The original and one copy of the Summons, but do not send the original if service is outside California.

If you decide to use a professional process server, look one up in the yellow pages of the phone book for the area near your spouse (big libraries and some phone companies keep national sets of phone books), or check with a process server in the area near you and see if they can recommend someone near your spouse. Call around for the best price. Call the one you select and discuss delivery of papers and the items they want sent.

If you are in no hurry, it may be cheaper to use a Sheriff, Marshal, or Constable. Just mail the items listed above to the office of one of those officials nearest your spouse, and request that they serve him. Also send a money order for $10 with a request to refund any unused portion. Be prepared to wait patiently for results.

If you decide to have a friend or relative make service (inside California only), deliver the items listed above and tell that person all they have to do is to personally hand the papers described in 8b to your spouse. If your spouse may possibly be a bit sticky about being served, the process server should know the following: Once your spouse has been located and identified, the server should say, "I have court papers for you." If your spouse won't open the door, or if he turns and runs, or in any other way tries to avoid service, the server can just put the papers in the nearest convenient spot where they can be picked up, then leave, and service will have been effectively completed.

Make sure the Proof of Service is filled out properly (see Chapter 9). If service is made outside California it must be proved by a sworn and notarized affidavit, so you should not send the original summons. Use only a professional or an official and request that he send his affidavit of service to you. Attach this to the Proof of Service when you file it.

8e   *Service by mail and acknowledgment*

If you know your spouse's address, and if your ex will cooperate to the extent of signing an Acknowledgment, then your job is easy. Someone (over 18, not you) must do the mailing for you.

A copy of the papers to be served (8b) should be mailed by first class mail, postage prepaid, to your spouse, together with the original and one copy of the Acknowledgement **and** a return envelope, postage prepaid, addressed to the sender.

An Acknowledgement form is provided with the forms in this book. Fill it out as shown in Fig. 7a. Make 3 copies.

All your spouse needs to do upon receipt of the papers is to enter the date they were received, then sign the original Acknowledgement, and return it to the sender. The other papers that were sent are not to be filled out or returned. The sender then completes the Proof of Service (Chapter 9) and the job is complete. Be sure to attach the original Acknowledgement to the Proof of Service when you file it. Service by this method is effective on the date the papers are signed by your spouse.

8f   *Service by certified or registered mail*

When you know your spouse's address and it is **outside** the state of California, you can serve papers by having someone (over 18, not you) mail the papers to be served (8b) via registered or certified mail, with a return receipt requested. Make sure you indicate "deliver to addressee only" on the post office form. When the return comes back with your spouse's signature, it must be filed as a part of the Proof of Service (Chapter 9). When using this method, the effective date of service is the 10th day after mailing. Use that date as the "date of service" on the forms and in court.

THE PROOF OF SERVICE

WHAT IT IS

This is a declaration swearing that certain steps were carried out to serve papers on the Respondent. It **must** be filed with the **original** Summons. If you lose or misplace the original Summons, you will need to prepare a Declaration of Service of Lost Summons (see note, Chapter 5).

HOW TO FILL IT OUT

As shown in Fig. 7. Prepare the original and one copy.

Note: Personal service (8d):

Make sure box 2c has been checked and the date of service entered on the front (Summons) side. If service is made in California by an official or a professional, send them the original Summons for them to fill out and return. If made by a friend, you can help fill it out, but they must sign it. If service is made outside California by an official or professional, do **not** send the original Summons. Request that they send you their notarized affidavit of service. You attach that to the original Summons and file it.

Note: Effective Date of Service:

1) Personal Service (8d) - the effective date of service is the day papers were handed to Respondent.

2) Service by mail and Acknowledgement (8e) - the effective date of service is the day Respondent signs the papers. Attach the original acknowledgement to the Proof of Service.

3) Service by certified or registered mail (8f) - the effective date of service is the 10th day after mailing. Attach the returned signature receipt to the Proof of Service.

4) Service by Publication - the effective date of service is 7 days after the last date of publication. See Appendix D.

---

if Respondent was served personally (8d) check box 2a then check box 1c and type in date, time and address of delivery.

if you served by method 8e or 8f check box 1d and indicate date and place of mailing.

check this box if you used method 8e. Attach completed Acknowledgment form.

check this box if you used method 8f. Attach return receipt.

check this box if friend serves or mails papers for you, and type in their name, address and phone under 6f.

enter amount or put in 'none'

check this box if you file in a county with a conciliation court. See Ch. 7.

type in Respondent's name as it appears on the Petition.

If other papers were served, check box 6 and specify: for example, the Decl. Re: Minors

Fill out Item 3 the same as Item 2 on the front (See p.54)

Signature of person making service, with date and place of signing.

Form content

PROOF OF SERVICE
(Use separate proof of service for each person served)

1 I served the Summons (Family Law) and Petition (Family Law) on respondent (name):
   a. with (1) ☐ blank Confidential Counseling Statement (5) ☐ completed and blank Property Declarations
           (2) ☐ Order to Show Cause and Application (6) ☐ Other (specify):
           (3) ☐ blank Responsive Declaration
           (4) ☐ completed and blank Income and
                 Expense Declarations
   b. ☐ By leaving copies with (name and title or relationship to person served):
   c. ☐ By delivery at ☐ home ☐ business
           (1) Date of: (3) Address:
           (2) Time of:
   d. ☐ By mailing
           (1) Date of: (2) Place of:

2. Manner of service: (Check proper box)
   a. ☐ Personal service. By personally delivering copies to the person served. (CCP 415.10)
   b. ☐ Substituted service on natural person, minor, incompetent. By leaving copies at the dwelling house, usual place of abode, or usual place of business of the person served in the presence of a competent member of the household or a person apparently in charge of the office or place of business, at least 18 years of age, who was informed of the general nature of the papers, and thereafter mailing (by first-class mail, postage prepaid) copies to the person served at the place where the copies were left. (CCP 415.20(b)) (Attach separate declaration or affidavit stating acts relied on to establish reasonable diligence in first attempting personal service.)
   c. ☐ Mail and acknowledgment service. By mailing (by first-class mail or airmail) copies to the person served, together with two copies of the form of notice and acknowledgment and a return envelope, postage prepaid, addressed to the sender. (CCP 415.30) (Attach completed acknowledgment of receipt.)
   d. ☐ Certified or registered mail service. By mailing to address outside California (by registered or certified airmail with return receipt requested) copies to the person served. (CCP 415.40) (Attach signed return receipt or other evidence of actual delivery to the person served.)
   e. ☐ Other (Specify code section):
           ☐ Additional page is attached.

3. The notice to the person served (Item 2 on the copy of the summons served) was completed as follows (CCP 412.30, 415.10, and 474):
   a. ☐ As an individual
   b. ☐ On behalf of Respondent
           Under: ☐ CCP 416.60 (Minor)   ☐ Other (specify):
                     ☐ CCP 416.70 (Ward or Conservatee)
                     ☐ CCP 416.90 (Individual)
   c. ☐ By personal delivery on (Date): . . . .
4. At the time of service I was at least 18 years of age and not a party to this action.
5. Fee for service: $ . . . .
6. Person serving
   a. ☐ Not a registered California process server.   e. ☐ California sheriff, marshal, or constable.
   b. ☐ Registered California process server.   f. Name, address and telephone number and
   c. ☐ Employee or independent contractor of a   if applicable, county of registration and number:
         registered California process server.
   d. ☐ Exempt from registration under Bus. & Prof.
         Code 22350(b)

   I declare under penalty of perjury that the foregoing   (For California sheriff, marshal or constable use)
   is true and correct and that this declaration is executed   I certify that the foregoing is true and correct and that
   on (date): . . . .   this certificate is executed on (date): . . . .
   at (place): . . . . , California.   at (place):

   _____   _____
          (Signature)   (Signature)

   A declaration under penalty of perjury must be signed in California or in a state that authorizes use of a declaration in place of an affidavit; otherwise an affidavit is required.

Figure 7a: HOW TO FILL OUT THE ACKNOWLEDGMENT

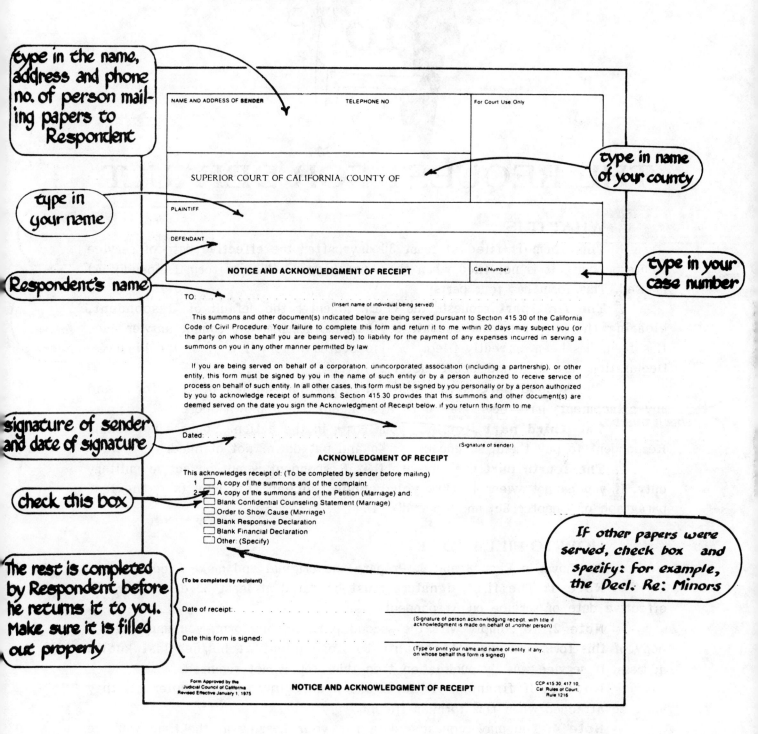

type in the name, address and phone no. of person mailing papers to Respondent

type in name of your county

type in your name

Respondent's name

type in your case number

signature of sender and date of signature

check this box

If other papers were served, check box and specify: for example, the Decl. Re: Minors

The rest is completed by Respondent before he returns it to you. Make sure it is filled out properly

NAME AND ADDRESS OF **SENDER**   TELEPHONE NO   For Court Use Only

SUPERIOR COURT OF CALIFORNIA, COUNTY OF

PLAINTIFF

DEFENDANT

NOTICE AND ACKNOWLEDGMENT OF RECEIPT   Case Number

TO:

(Insert name of individual being served)

This summons and other document(s) indicated below are being served pursuant to Section 415.30 of the California Code of Civil Procedure. Your failure to complete this form and return it to me within 20 days may subject you (or the party on whose behalf you are being served) to liability for the payment of any expenses incurred in serving a summons on you in any other manner permitted by law

If you are being served on behalf of a corporation, unincorporated association (including a partnership), or other entity, this form must be signed by you in the name of such entity or by a person authorized to receive service of process on behalf of such entity. In all other cases, this form must be signed by you personally or by a person authorized by you to acknowledge receipt of summons. Section 415.30 provides that this summons and other document(s) are deemed served on the date you sign the Acknowledgment of Receipt below, if you return this form to me

Dated: _____   _____
                                        (Signature of sender)

ACKNOWLEDGMENT OF RECEIPT

This acknowledges receipt of: (To be completed by sender before mailing)
1 ☐ A copy of the summons and of the complaint
2 ☐ A copy of the summons and of the Petition (Marriage) and
    ☐ Blank Confidential Counseling Statement (Marriage)
    ☐ Order to Show Cause (Marriage)
    ☐ Blank Responsive Declaration
    ☐ Blank Financial Declaration
    ☐ Other: (Specify)

(To be completed by recipient)

Date of receipt: ....   _____
                                        (Signature of person acknowledging receipt, with title if
                                        acknowledgment is made on behalf of another person)

Date this form is signed: ....   _____
                                        (Type or print your name and name of entity, if any,
                                        on whose behalf this form is signed)

Form Approved by the   **NOTICE AND ACKNOWLEDGMENT OF RECEIPT**   CCP 415.30, 417.10,
Judicial Council of California   Cal. Rules of Court,
Revised Effective January 1, 1975   Rule 1216

THE PROOF OF SERVICE   85

THE REQUEST FOR DEFAULT

WHAT IT IS

This form is filed at least 30 days after the effective date of service on Respondent. It is not filed when the Appearance & Waiver form (Appendix A) is used. This form has four parts:

The first part requests the Clerk to enter the default of Respondent, clearing the way for your uncontested hearing. Respondent cannot answer once this form has been correctly filed. It also states which, if any, of the Financial Declarations are attached (see Chapter 11).

The second part is your oath, swearing that copies of this form and any attachments have been mailed to Respondent's last known address.

The third part itemizes your costs in the action. You are not asking Respondent to pay them, so check box 4a and put down "not claimed."

The fourth part is your oath that Respondent is not on active military duty. If you cannot swear to this, you cannot proceed this way (see the last paragraph of Chapter 8c, and Appendix A).

HOW TO FILL IT OUT

As shown in Figs. 8 and 9. Prepare the original and make 3 copies.

Note 1: The first signature **must** be dated at least 30 days after the effective date of service on Respondent.

Note 2: To comply with the second part of this form, you must mail a copy of this form and any attachments to Respondent at his/her last known address. If service was by publication then this step is not required.

Note 3: If financial declarations are required (see Chapter 11) they must be attached when this form is filed.

Note 4: You may request a date for your hearing at the time you file this form, or at a later time.

Figure 8: HOW TO FILL OUT THE REQUEST FOR DEFAULT

type in caption as shown in chapter 1

check box for whichever form IS attached, if any.

check box for whichever form is NOT attached, then check box 1-4 to explain why: check (1) if a _completed_ form was attached to the Petition. check (2) if there is a written agreement. check (3) and/or (4) if you are NOT requesting any order which makes the form relevant.

type in case number.

type in name and date of signing. See text note.

your signature.

if you served Respondent by publication, check box a, otherwise check box b and type in date you mailed him this form and his last known address. See text note.

type in name, date and place of signing. See 1f.

your signature.

ATTORNEY OR PARTY WITHOUT ATTORNEY (NAME AND ADDRESS):   TELEPHONE NO   FOR COURT USE ONLY

ATTORNEY FOR (NAME)

SUPERIOR COURT OF CALIFORNIA, COUNTY OF
STREET ADDRESS
MAILING ADDRESS
CITY AND ZIP CODE
BRANCH NAME

MARRIAGE OF
PETITIONER

RESPONDENT

REQUEST TO ENTER DEFAULT   CASE NUMBER

1. TO THE CLERK: Please enter the default of the respondent who has failed to respond to the petition.
2. A completed ☐ Income and Expense Declaration   ☐ Property Declaration is attached.
3. A completed ☐ Income and Expense Declaration   ☐ Property Declaration is *not* attached because (check at least one of the following)
   (1) ☐ There have been no changes since the previous filing
   (2) ☐ The issues subject to disposition by the court in this proceeding are the subject of a written agreement.
   (3) ☐ There are no issues of child custody, child or spousal support, division of community property or attorney fees and costs subject to determination by this court.
   (4) ☐ The petition does not request money, property, costs or attorney fees.

Dated:

_____   _____
(Type or print name)   Signature of (Attorney for) Petitioner

3. DECLARATION
   a. ☐ No mailing is required because service was by publication and the address of respondent remains unknown.
   b. ☐ A copy of this Request to Enter Default including any attachments was mailed to the respondent's attorney of record or, if none, to respondent's last known address as follows
      (1) Date of mailing: (2) Addressed as follows:

   c. I declare under penalty of perjury that the foregoing is true and correct and that this declaration is executed on (date): . . . . at (place): . . . . , California.

_____   _____
(Type or print name)   (Signature of declarant)

FOR COURT USE ONLY
Default entered as requested on (date):
                                    Clerk, by:
Default NOT entered. Reason:

(See reverse for Memorandum of Costs and Declaration of Nonmilitary Status)

The declaration under penalty of perjury must be signed in California or in a state that authorizes use of a declaration in place of an affidavit; otherwise an affidavit is required. (CCP 2015.5)

Form Adopted by Rule 1286
Judicial Council of California
Revised Effective January 1, 1980

**REQUEST TO ENTER DEFAULT
(FAMILY LAW)**   CCP 585,587

Figure 9: # HOW TO FILL OUT THE REQUEST FOR DEFAULT

check this box

4. MEMORANDUM OF COSTS

a. ☐ Costs and disbursements are waived.
b. Costs and disbursements are listed as follows

(1) ☐ Clerk's fees . . . . $ . . . .

(2) ☐ Process server's fees . . . . $ . . . .

(3) ☐ Other (specify) . . . . $ . . . .

. . . . $ . . . .

. . . . $ . . . .

. . . . $ . . . .

TOTAL . . . . $ . . . .

type in "Not Claimed"

I am the attorney, agent, or party who claims these costs. To the best of my knowledge and belief the foregoing items of cost are correct and have been necessarily incurred in this cause or proceeding.

I declare under penalty of perjury that the foregoing is true and correct and that this declaration is executed on (date): . . . . at (place): . . . . , California.

type in name, date and place of signing. See 1f.

. . . .
(Type or print name)   (Signature of declarant)

your signature

5. DECLARATION OF NONMILITARY STATUS

Respondent is not in the military service or in the military service of the United States as defined in Section 101 of the Soldiers' and Sailors' Relief Act of 1940, as amended, and not entitled to the benefits of such act.

I declare under penalty of perjury that the foregoing is true and correct and that this declaration is executed on (date): . . . . at (place): . . . . , California.

type in name, date and place of signing. See 1f.

. . . .
(Type or print name)   (Signature of declarant)

your signature

THE FINANCIAL DECLARATIONS

WHAT THEY ARE

The Financial Declarations are **two** forms which are designed to give the judge details of your finances. In general, they **must** be filed whenever the information is relevant to any order you are seeking:

1. If your petition requests support, you **must** file the Income and Expense Declaration.

2. If your Petition requests a division of property (Petition, Item 4c or 4d), then the Property Declaration **must** be filed.

3. If your Petition does not request either support or property orders, then these forms are **not** filed.

4. If you come into court with a written agreement (see Chapter E), then the Property Declaration need not be filed. If there is child support in the agreement, then you should file the Income and Expense Declaration.

If either of the Financial Declarations are to be filed, they should be attached to and filed with the Request for Default form unless they have been previously completed and filed with the Petition.

HOW TO FILL THEM OUT

Make an extra copy of the **blank** forms to use as work sheets. Fill them out as shown in Figs. 10, 11, 12 and 13. The forms are detailed and nearly self-explanatory. Prepare the original and 3 copies.

Property Declaration: The 1st column calls for the amount you can get for the item or group of items if you have to sell on the open market. Check ads, talk to dealers, try to estimate what you could get. The judge might ask how you arrived at your figures. In the 2nd column put the amount of any debt on the item or group of items, deduct from the 1st column and enter the balance in the 3rd column. In the 4th and 5th columns, put the value of property as you propose it to be divided between you and Respondent. The total value, considering all debts and property, should come out about equal, unless you fit the exception described in Chapter B4. **Note:** If you run out of room on this form, go to the clerk and get a "Continuation of Property Declaration" sheet.

Income and Expense Declaration: Items 1-11 are for income, 12-21 are for deductions. If you know the figures for Respondent, put them in, otherwise put "est." when you are estimating, or "unk." for "unknown" where you have no idea at all. Get as much information as you can as the judge cannot make an order without something to go on.

Note: Every column should have an entry. Put down the correct figure, unk., or N/A for those parts which are not relevant.

Figure 10:
HOW TO FILL OUT THE PROPERTY DECLARATION
(front)

type in caption as shown in chapter 1

check these boxes

type in your case number

type in requested information. See Ch. B8 and text notes.

ATTORNEY OR PARTY WITHOUT ATTORNEY (NAME AND ADDRESS)	TELEPHONE NO	FOR COURT USE ONLY

ATTORNEY FOR (NAME)

SUPERIOR COURT OF CALIFORNIA, COUNTY OF
STREET ADDRESS
MAILING ADDRESS
CITY AND ZIP CODE
BRANCH NAME

MARRIAGE OF
PETITIONER

RESPONDENT

☐ PETITIONER'S ☐ RESPONDENT'S
☐ COMMUNITY & QUASI-COMMUNITY PROPERTY DECLARATION
☐ SEPARATE PROPERTY DECLARATION

CASE NUMBER

INSTRUCTIONS

When this form is attached to Petition or Response, values and your proposal regarding division need not be completed. Do not list community, including quasi-community, property with separate property on the same form. Quasi-community property must be so identified. For additional space, use the form ''Continuation of Property Declaration.''

ITEM NO	BRIEF DESCRIPTION	GROSS FAIR MARKET VALUE	AMOUNT OF DEBT	NET FAIR MARKET VALUE	PROPOSAL FOR DIVISION AWARD TO	
					PETITIONER	RESPONDENT
		$	$	$	$	$
1.	REAL ESTATE					
2.	HOUSEHOLD FURNITURE, FURNISHINGS, APPLIANCES					
3.	JEWELRY, ANTIQUES, ART, COIN COLLECTIONS, etc.					
4.	VEHICLES, BOATS, TRAILERS					
5.	SAVINGS, CHECKING, CREDIT UNION, CASH					

(Continued on reverse)

The declaration under penalty of perjury must be signed in California or in a state that authorizes use of a declaration in place of an affidavit, otherwise an affidavit is required.

Form Adopted by Rule 1285.55
Judicial Council of California
Effective January 1, 1980

**PROPERTY DECLARATION
(FAMILY LAW)**

Figure 11:

HOW TO FILL OUT THE PROPERTY DECLARATION
(back)

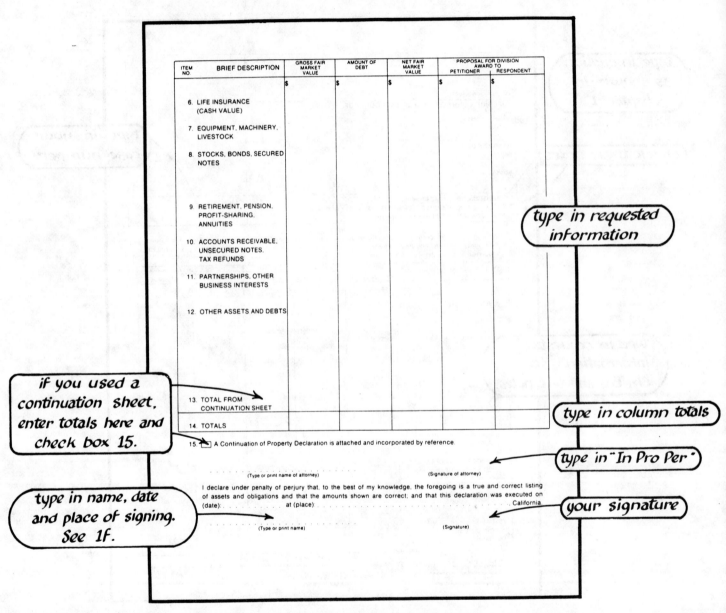

type in requested information

if you used a continuation sheet, enter totals here and check box 15.

type in column totals

type in "In Pro Per"

type in name, date and place of signing. See 1f.

your signature

NOTE: If you run out of room on this form, go to the clerk and get a "Continuation of Property Declaration sheet".

Figure 12:

HOW TO FILL OUT THE INCOME & EXPENSE DECLARATION
(front)

type in caption as shown in chapter 1

type in case number

check this box

fill in requested information. See text note.

ATTORNEY OR PARTY WITHOUT ATTORNEY (NAME AND ADDRESS):   TELEPHONE NO: FOR COURT USE ONLY

ATTORNEY FOR (NAME)

SUPERIOR COURT OF CALIFORNIA, COUNTY OF
STREET ADDRESS
MAILING ADDRESS
CITY AND ZIP CODE
BRANCH NAME

MARRIAGE OF
PETITIONER

RESPONDENT

INCOME AND EXPENSE DECLARATION
☐ PETITIONER   ☐ RESPONDENT   CASE NUMBER:

GROSS MONTHLY INCOME	Petitioner	Respondent	DEDUCTIONS FROM GROSS INCOME	Petitioner	Respondent
1 Salary & wages (Include commissions, bonuses and overtime)	$	$	12. State income taxes	$	$
			13. Federal income taxes	$	$
2 Pensions & retirement	$	$	14. Social Security	$	$
3 Social Security	$	$	15. State disability insurance	$	$
4 Disability and unemployment benefits	$	$			
5 Public assistance (Welfare, AFDC payments, etc)	$	$	16. Medical and other insurance	$	$
6 Child/spousal support	$	$	17. Union and other dues	$	$
7 Dividends and interest	$	$	18. Retirement and pension fund	$	$
8 Rents (gross receipts, less cash expenses, attach schedule)	$	$	19. Savings plan	$	$
9 Contributions to household expenses from other sources	$	$	20. Other deductions (Specify)	$	$
10 Income from all other sources (gross receipts, less cash expenses, attach schedule)	$	$	21. TOTAL DEDUCTIONS	$	$
			11. TOTAL GROSS MONTHLY INCOME (from line 11)	$	$
			21. TOTAL DEDUCTIONS (From line 21)	$	$
11 TOTAL GROSS MONTHLY INCOME	$	$	22. NET MONTHLY INCOME (line 11 minus line 21)	$	$

23. Withholding information   a. Number of exemptions claimed: b. Marital status:

24. Certain property under the control of the parties

	Petitioner	Respondent		Petitioner	Respondent
a Cash & checking accounts	$	$	c. Stocks, bonds, life insurance, other liquid assets	$	$
b Savings & credit union accounts	$	$	d. TOTAL (24a,b,c)	$	$

The declaration under penalty of perjury must be signed in California or in a state that authorizes use of a declaration in place of an affidavit, otherwise an affidavit is required.

Form Adopted by Rule 1285.50
Judicial Council of California
Revised Effective January 1, 1980

INCOME & EXPENSE DECLARATION
(FAMILY LAW)

NOTE: on the Income and Expense Declaration put an entry on every line, either a figure, or 0, or "unk." for unknown.

HOW TO FILL OUT THE INCOME & EXPENSE DECLARATION
(back)

25. List the name, age, and relationship of all members of the household whose expenses are included below

MONTHLY EXPENSES	Petitioner	Respondent			Petitioner	Respondent
26. Residence payments			34. Child/spousal support (prior marriage)		$	$
a. Rent or mortgage	$	$				
b. Taxes & insurance	$	$	35. School		$	$
c. Maintenance	$	$	36. Entertainment		$	$
27. Food & household supplies	$	$	37. Incidentals		$	$
28. Utilities & telephone	$	$	38. Transportation & auto expenses (insurance, gas, oil, repair)		$	$
29. Laundry & cleaning	$	$	39. Installment payments (insert total and itemize below at 42)	$	$	
30. Clothing	$	$				
31. Medical & dental	$	$				
32. Insurance (life, health accident, etc.)	$	$	40. Other (specify)		$	$
33. Child care	$	$	41. TOTAL MONTHLY EXPENSES		$	$

(callout) fill in requested information.

42. ITEMIZATION OF INSTALLMENT PAYMENTS OR OTHER DEBTS ☐ Continued on attachment 42

CREDITOR'S NAME	FOR	MONTHLY PAYMENT	BALANCE
		$	$

43. ☐ ATTORNEY FEES HAVE BEEN REQUESTED

a. I have paid my attorney for fees and costs the sum of $ . . . . b. My arrangement for attorney fees and costs is:

_____   _____
(Print or type name of Attorney)   (Signature of Attorney)

(callout) type in "In Pro Per"

I declare under penalty of perjury that the foregoing, including any attachment, is true and correct and that this declaration is executed at (place): . . . . , California, on (date): . . . .

_____   _____
(Print or type name of Declarant)   (Signature of Declarant)

(callout) type in name, date and place of signing.

(callout) your signature

---

94   THE FINANCIAL DECLARATIONS

THE HEARING

In order to get your dissolution, you either have to go to a hearing, or file an Affidavit in Lieu of Testimony (see Appendix C). Going personally to the hearing is preferred in most cases, and is easier than you may think. Since your spouse has not responded and will not be in court, you will have an "uncontested" hearing. It will be very brief, almost a mere formality. Most of your time will be spent waiting for it to start, so don't worry. You won't be grilled - the judge just wants all the facts. Follow these instructions and you'll have no problem.

12a *Requesting the hearing*

To get a date for your hearing, you have to ask the Clerk's Office to "set" your case on their trial calendar. If you want to avoid extra delay from the 60 day appeal period (see Chapter A10), then you should have the hearing sometime within 4 months of the service of process.

The time and manner of requesting a hearing varies from county to county, so ask your Clerk's Office when and how it is done in your county. Do they have local forms? Extra fees? When do they want the Interlocutory Judgment and Notice of Entry? In some counties, you merely call them on the phone anytime after they receive your second papers, but many counties require a local form to be filed when you request a hearing. Some counties also want

---

THE HEARING 95

the Interlocutory Judgment and Notice of Entry at this time, others do not. There are two local forms at the end of this chapter for illustration, but if you run into one which is different and you can't figure out how to do it, just send two blank copies to Nolo Press with a stamped, self-addressed envelope and we will send instructions.

If you can take the time, it can be very helpful to go watch some uncontested divorces on some day before your own hearing. This will give you a good idea of what to expect when your case comes up, what sort your judge is, how the courtroom is run. Ask your Clerk when uncontested dissolutions are generally heard.

12b | *The day of the hearing*

Appearances might count, so dress cleanly and neatly. If you own any, wear business-type clothing. Get to the courthouse a little before your case is scheduled to give yourself time to find the right place.

Most counties have more than one Superior Court judge. Each judge has his own courtroom, called a "department," which is identified by a number or letter. In some counties you go straight to the assigned department for your hearing. In larger counties, you may go first to a "presiding" or "master calendar" department. In such a case, go there and listen for the name of your case to be called, stand up and answer, "Ready!" and your case will then be sent to some other department for the hearing. Sometimes they will want you to pick up your file and carry it to the hearing - find out by asking the clerk or bailiff when you appear for the hearing, or call and ask the clerk ahead of time.

When you get to the proper courtroom for your hearing, tell the clerk or bailiff that you are present. If you haven't already filed them, hand the clerk the original and three copies of the Interlocutory Judgment (Chapter 13), and the Notice of Entry of Judgment (Chapter 14). While waiting for your case to be called, you may get to watch others go before you. See how easy it is?

When your case is called, answer "Ready!." Go right on up, get sworn, and take the stand. Take time to arrange yourself and your papers. Relax. Some judges will ask you questions to get the information they want, but most will just tell you to begin. Tell the judge facts and information about your case and the orders you want made. Always call the judge "Your Honor."

The outline below is your guide - use the portions of it which apply to you. Don't take this book to the stand, but **do** make complete notes or cut out these pages and take them up with you. Check off each item as you give it in court to make sure you don't skip over and forget to say any part of it. Take your time. If the judge asks questions, it is only in order to become better informed and be satisfied that justice, as he or she understands it, is being done. Don't worry, just answer **briefly** exactly what is asked. Don't volunteer information that is not asked for.

I. IN EVERY CASE, GIVE THE FOLLOWING INFORMATION:

A. Your Honor, my name is _____, and I am the Petitioner is this case.

B. All of the facts stated in my Petition are true and correct.

C. (I/Respondent) resided in California for more than six months, and in (County your court is in) County for more than three months, immediately prior to the filing of the Petition.

D. Using exactly these words, tell the judge: "During the course of our marriage, there arose irreconcilable differences which led to the irremediable breakdown of our marriage. There is no chance for a reconciliation. Your honor, I ask that the marriage be dissolved."

II. CONTINUE, USING THE PORTIONS THAT APPLY TO YOUR CASE:

A. CHILDREN:

1. None: Your Honor, the Respondent and I have no minor children, and none are expected.

2. If you have children:

    a. Your Honor, the Respondent and I have __ child(ren): (Give the full name, age, and birthdate of each).

    b. Custody: I know that (I am/Respondent is/Respondent and I are both) fit and proper to have custody of the child(ren), and it would be in the child(ren)'s best interest to have the care, custody and control of the child(ren) awarded to (me/Respondent/us both jointly).

    c. Visitation:

        i. If you have requested joint custody, say nothing, visitation is not applicable.

        ii. If you are satisfied to have rights of reasonable visitation ordered, add "...subject to the right of reasonable visitation to be awarded to (Respondent/Petitioner)."

        iii. If you want visits ordered for specific days and hours, say "Visitation should be ordered according to a set schedule, because (tell the facts which make this necessary). Therefore, I request that visitation be ordered to take place (state the schedule you would like to have ordered)."

B. CHILD SUPPORT AND SPOUSAL SUPPORT:

1. No children and no request for spousal support:

    a. Where Petitioner is the wife: Your Honor, I do not need or want spousal support, and I understand that if I do not ask for it now I lose all right to it forever.

    b. Where Petitioner is the husband: You will need a written waiver of spousal support from Respondent (see Chapter D), otherwise plan on an award of at least $1 per month. If the waiver is part of a larger marital settlement agreement, say nothing at this time. If all you have is a waiver of spousal support, hand the original to the judge and say, "I recognize the signature on this waiver of spousal support to be that of Respondent, and I request that it be admitted into evidence."

2. If you want spousal support and/or child support:

    a. "The information in the Income & Expense Declaration(s) is true and accurate to the best of my knowledge and belief." This should be enough, but the judge may want you to go into it in more detail, so be prepared to talk about it a little bit. Don't worry, just tell it the best you can, using the financial declaration as your guide.

b. I request that (Petitioner/Respondent) be ordered to pay to (Respondent/Petitioner) $____ per month for spousal support, to continue until _____.

c. I request that (Petitioner/Respondent) be ordered to pay to (Respondent/Petitioner) $____ per month per child for child support, a total of $____ per month. If support is to continue beyond the age of 18, that must be stated here. If the child is being supported with welfare funds (AFDC), say "(I am/Respondent is) receiving welfare to help support the child(ren), so support payments are to be made through (title of officer for your county).

d. If you want an order on life/health insurance or payment of necessary medical/dental bills for spouse or children, then ask for it here.

C. PROPERTY AND BILLS:

1. None: If you checked box 4a on the Petition, then tell the judge, "There is no property subject to disposition by the court."

2. Divided by agreement: If you checked box 4b on the Petition, then say, "Your Honor, the original copy of the marital settlement agreement has been submitted with the Interlocutory Judgment. My signature is on it, and I recognize the other signature as that of Respondent. I ask that it be admitted into evidence. I request that...

Los Angeles County: ...the court make the orders set out in the Interlocutory Judgment which I have submitted for your signature, and which are the same as the parts of the marital settlement agreement which remain to be performed in the future.

Other counties: ...the marital settlement agreement be approved and incorporated into the Interlocutory Judgment by reference, and that the parties be ordered to comply with its terms and conditions.

3. Divided by the Court: If you checked box 4c or 4d on the Petition, then tell the judge, "The information in the Property Declaration is true, accurate, and complete, to the best of my knowledge and belief. I request that the property be divided as set forth in the Interlocutory Judgment which has been submitted for Your Honor's signature." Be prepared to answer questions about the property or your requested division of it if the judge wants to go into things in more detail.

Pension plans: If there is a community interest in a pension or retirement plan, take care of it by one of the following methods (see Chapter B3c):

a) Trade-off: The pension is listed and valued along with the other property in the Property Declaration. Say nothing unless the judge asks questions.

b) Waiver by Petitioner: Tell the judge, "Your Honor, I know I may have some right to part of Respondent's pension plan which is listed in the Property declaration, but I have thought it over and I don't want or need any part of it. I waive any and all rights I may have in Respondent's pension plan."

c) Written waiver by Respondent: Hand the judge the original and one copy of the waiver and say, "Your Honor, this is Respondent's waiver of rights to my pension plan. I recognize the signature as the Respondent's. Would you please admit this into evidence?"

d) Reserved for the future: Say, "Your Honor, I request that the court reserve jurisdiction to decide the matter of (Respondent's/ Petitioner's) pension plan at a future time, as set forth in the Interlocutory Decree."

4. Separate property: If you used Item 5 in the Petition, then say, "The property listed under item 5 of the Petition is separate property, and I ask that it be confirmed as such." The judge may want to ask questions about how some item was acquired, so be prepared, and bring any related documents you may have.

D. RESTORATION OF WIFE'S MAIDEN NAME:

Your Honor, (Petitioner/Respondent) wants her former name restored as set forth in the Interlocutory Judgment.

E. CONCLUSION: Your Honor, that concludes my statement.

When your testimony is completed, the judge will recite an Interlocutory Order. You then step down. You do not need any witnesses.

The written Interlocutory Judgment which you have prepared **must** correspond to the judge's spoken order. If it does not, get it back from the clerk, change it to make it accurate, and file it later. The clerk may hand you your copy of the Interlocutory Judgment. If he does not, it will be mailed to you, as will your copy of the Notice of Entry.

12c | *Trouble Shooting Guide*

We said it before and say it again: 99 times out of 100 there will be no trouble with a hearing. However, it will make you feel better if you know what to do just in case you are that unfortunate 1 out of the 100.

1. Before the hearing begins:

It sometimes happens that the people who work in the court forget that they are there to serve the public. It usually does no good to remind them. Rather, if the clerk or bailiff (or even the judge) is less than helpful or polite, just keep calm, be nice, and quietly but firmly pursue your goal. You have a right to be there and a right to represent yourself.

If someone is making things difficult for you, it is very possible that there is a reason. If so, you must find it out and correct the problem. Ask what is the matter, and at least try to get some hint about the general area of the problem. If necessary, ask to speak to another clerk or to their supervisor. Don't

---

get upset. What is important is to correct the problem. Go over this book and double check everything. You can always return to the Clerk's Office or to court another day.

2. After your hearing begins:

This is a scary time for something to go wrong, but don't worry, you have an excellent escape hatch (or panic button) that you can use if all else fails. Lawyers use it all the time. It is called the continuance.

If the judge is very difficult, or refuses to grant your dissolution, this means he or she thinks you have left out something essential. Ask the judge, politely, to explain, as it is likely that you can give additional testimony that will solve the problem. If things go very wrong and you can't figure out what your problem is, or if you get into any kind of situation you can't handle, just tell the judge, "Your Honor, I request that this matter be taken off calendar, to be reset for hearing at another time, so that I may have time to seek advice and further prepare this case for presentation." During the next recess, see if the clerk or bailiff can help you, or ask to see the judge in chambers. Go over this book and double check everything.

Assuming you figure out what went wrong, have your case set for hearing again, just like you did the first time, and do the hearing over again. If you think the problem was personal to that judge, ask the clerk if there is an informal way to avoid a judge who doesn't seem to like you or people who represent themselves. If you are really up against the wall, it is possible to file an Affidavit of Prejudice (one time only) and force them to give you another judge. This should be regarded as an extreme emergency measure, not likely to create good will for you at the courthouse.

3. After the hearing:

If the judge grants your dissolution but refuses to sign your Interlocutory Judgment, this means the judge thinks there is something wrong with it. Probably it is different from the orders announced in court. Ask the clerk what is wrong (or look at the clerk's docket sheet, a public record) and make up a new Interlocutory Judgment form. Do it as soon as possible, and bring it in for the judge's signature.

REQUEST FOR DEFAULT SETTING

(Used in Los Angeles County)

type caption as shown in chapter 1

NAME, ADDRESS, AND TELEPHONE OF ATTORNEY(S)

ATTORNEY(S) FOR:

SUPERIOR COURT OF CALIFORNIA, COUNTY OF LOS ANGELES

In Re the Marriage of

CASE NUMBER

AND

PETITIONER,

RESPONDENT.

REQUEST FOR DEFAULT SETTING
(Domestic Relations and Branch District Civil Actions)

TO THE CLERK OF THE COURT:

Request is hereby made that the within matter for (Check appropriate box or boxes)

☒ DISSOLUTION ☐ NULLITY ☐ LEGAL SEPARATION

☐ _____ (Other)

☐ CIVIL ACTION (For setting in branch district court only)

be set for trial on the default calendar. Estimated time for trial is ...... **15 minutes**

DATED: ....✓........................ SIGNED **(your signature) in pro per**
(Attorney for moving party)

CLERK'S MEMORANDUM

The said case was on .... set for trial for ....

at .... o'clock ..... M. in Dept. ....

☐ FIRST SETTING ☐ RESET ☐ LAST HEARD IN DEPT.

Notice of trial date and department sent by U.S. mail to moving attorney, on ....
....

23 7oK347K—(Rev. 7-70)— Cdb 6-74

DEPUTY COUNTY CLERK

NOTICE OF TRIAL SETTING

Moving Attorney will please fill in case title and number, and his mailing address in the spaces provided below.

CASE TITLE: **Your name**
Respondent's name

SUPERIOR COURT NO. **Your case #**

Please take notice that the within matter has been set for trial as a default, on ....
19 ...... at ...... M, in Dept, ... of the Superior Court.

CLARENCE E. CABELL, COUNTY CLERK

By _____
Deputy

Name **Your name**

Address **and address**

City _____

REQUEST FOR DEFAULT OR UNCONTESTED HEARING

*(Used in El Dorado, Placer, San Joaquin,
Yolo, Solano, Sutter, and Butte counties)*

Name, Address and Telephone Number of Attorney(s)

Space Below for Use of Court Clerk Only

type caption as shown in chapter 1

Attorney(s) for_____

SUPERIOR COURT OF CALIFORNIA, COUNTY OF_____

In re the marriage of

CASE NUMBER

Petitioner: and

REQUEST FOR DEFAULT OR
UNCONTESTED HEARING
(Marriage)

Respondent:

Check this box & put in date of filing if you use Request for Default form.

To the Clerk: Please place this proceeding on the court's default or uncontested Family Law Calendar for hearing on
_____ (Date to be inserted by clerk.)

This may be heard as uncontested matter because:

☐ Default of Respondent was entered on (Date): _____
☐ Appearance and waiver was filed by Respondent on (Date): _____
☐ Response and waiver was filed by Respondent on (Date): _____

Check this box & put in date of filing if you used Appearance & Waiver instead of Service of process.

There is (not) _____ a property settlement agreement. If so, a copy:

☐ Was filed on (Date): _____
☐ Is attached.

Indicate where you attached the Interlocutory Judgement

The proposed Interlocutory Judgment:

☐ Is attached to the (Petition/Response/Appearance and Waiver): _____
☐ Is attached.

This matter will be personally presented in court by attorney _____

Petitioner, in pro per

date of your signature

Date : _____

Please note below your suggested hearing dates.

_____

_____

put in some convenient dates or "anytime"

in Pro per
(Name of Law Firm)

By **Your signature**
(Signature of Attorney)

Type your name
(Type or print name)

Type in "not" if there is no property agreement.

If there is a written agreement, cross out "not" and fill out this section.

PLEASE FILE IN DUPLICATE
Your copy of this request will be returned with
the hearing date filled in.

Approved by Third District
Superior Courts 7/1/71

REQUEST FOR DEFAULT OR UNCONTESTED HEARING (Marriage)

FORM 7.3(b)

THE INTERLOCUTORY JUDGMENT

WHAT IT IS

When you are in court for your hearing, the judge will speak his order. But **note** that the order will **not** become effective until it is first put in writing, signed by the judge, **and** entered in the Clerk's records.

The Interlocutory Order does not actually dissolve your marriage - it just clears the way for it to be dissolved later. All other portions of the Interlocutory Order, such as those concerning child custody, support, property, etc., become effective immediately.

It is very important that the written Interlocutory Judgment match the order spoken by the judge, otherwise he will not sign it. Since you almost always get what you ask for in uncontested cases, you should prepare the Interlocutory Judgment ahead of time. However, if there are any changes to be made - if the judge orders something different from what is in your prepared form - then get the forms back from the clerk, make the necessary changes, and return them for the judge's signature.

HOW TO FILL IT OUT

Fill out the Interlocutory Judgment as shown in Fig. 14. Prepare the original and 3 copies.

Note: The court acquired jurisdiction of Respondent on the date that service of process became effective (see Chapter 9 notes).

Note: If your case has children, support to be ordered, or property to be divided, you will have to add further orders to suit your own situation. See the instructions below, "HOW TO ADD FURTHER ORDERS."

---

type caption as shown in chapter 1

type in your case number

type in date of hearing. Also put in your judge's name and department or room number, if you know it.

check this box

check this box

if you filed the Request for Default, check box a, and type in effective date of service. If you used the Appearance and Waiver, check box b, and type in date it was filed.

check this box if there are further orders

check this box if wife's former name to be restored and type in name in full exactly as she wishes it to be.

if there are more orders check this box, check box below judge's signature line, put number of attached pages at item 5.

Form text on the judgment:

ATTORNEY OR PARTY WITHOUT ATTORNEY (NAME AND ADDRESS) — TELEPHONE NO — FOR COURT USE ONLY

ATTORNEY FOR (NAME)

SUPERIOR COURT OF CALIFORNIA, COUNTY OF
STREET ADDRESS
MAILING ADDRESS
CITY AND ZIP CODE
BRANCH NAME

MARRIAGE OF
PETITIONER

RESPONDENT

INTERLOCUTORY JUDGMENT OF DISSOLUTION OF MARRIAGE — CASE NUMBER

1. This proceeding came on for ☐ default or uncontested ☐ contested hearing as follows.
   a. Date: ☐ Dept. ☐ Div. ☐ Room:
   b. Judge (name): ☐ Temporary judge
   c. ☐ Petitioner present in court ☐ Attorney present in court (name):
   d. ☐ Respondent present in court ☐ Attorney present in court (name):
   e. ☐ Claimant present in court ☐ Attorney present in court (name):

2. The court acquired jurisdiction of the respondent on (date):
   a. ☐ Respondent was served with process.
   b. ☐ Respondent appeared.

3. THE COURT ORDERS
   a. An interlocutory judgment be entered and the parties are entitled to have their marriage dissolved.
   b. After six months from the date the court acquired jurisdiction of the respondent a final judgment of dissolution may be entered upon proper application of either party or on the court's own motion, unless a dismissal signed by both parties is filed. The final judgment shall include such other and further relief as may be necessary to a complete disposition of this proceeding, but entry of the final judgment shall not deprive this court of its jurisdiction over any matter expressly reserved to it in this or the final judgment until a final disposition is made of each such matter.
   c. Jurisdiction is reserved to make such other and further orders as may be necessary to carry out the provisions of this judgment.

4. ☐ THE COURT FURTHER ORDERS
   a. ☐ Wife's former name be restored (specify):
   b. ☐ Other:

Dated: . . . .

Judge of the Superior Court

5. Total number of pages attached: ☐ Signature follows last attachment

THIS INTERLOCUTORY JUDGMENT DOES NOT CONSTITUTE A FINAL DISSOLUTION OF MARRIAGE AND THE PARTIES ARE STILL MARRIED. ONE OF THE PARTIES MUST SUBMIT A REQUEST FOR FINAL JUDGMENT ON THE FORM PRESCRIBED BY RULE 1288. NEITHER PARTY MAY REMARRY UNTIL A FINAL JUDGMENT OF DISSOLUTION IS ENTERED.

ALTHOUGH AN OBLIGATION BASED ON A CONTRACT IS ASSIGNED TO ONE PARTY AS PART OF THE DIVISION OF THE COMMUNITY, IF THE PARTY TO WHOM THE OBLIGATION WAS ASSIGNED DEFAULTS ON THE CONTRACT, THE CREDITOR MAY HAVE A CAUSE OF ACTION AGAINST THE OTHER PARTY.

No attachment permitted on less than a full page. Cal Rule of Ct 201(b)

Form Adopted by Rule 1287
Judicial Council of California
Revised Effective January 1, 1981

INTERLOCUTORY JUDGMENT OF DISSOLUTION OF MARRIAGE (FAMILY LAW)

CC 4512, 4514

HOW TO ADD FURTHER ORDERS:

If you want the court to make orders regarding custody, support, or property, you will need to add more wording. Fill out items 4 and 5 as shown in Fig. 14. Type "continued on next page" on the judge's signature line. Put the rest of your orders on 8 1/2 x 11 sheets of white paper with the heading "Continuation of Judgment" typed at the top of each sheet. Double space. Always refer to the parties as "Petitioner" and "Respondent." Use only one side of each sheet. At the end of your orders type in a line for the date and judge's signature just like the one on the official form.

Below is a guide for you to use in preparing your orders. Use the parts that apply to your case and change the wording to fit your particular situation.

A. CHILDREN: If there are children, use **both** of the following orders for child custody and support:

It is further ordered that the care, custody and control of the minor child(ren) of the parties:

(list full name and date of birth of each child)

is awarded to (Petitioner and Respondent, jointly/ Petitioner/ Respondent/ other) subject to the right of reasonable visitation which is hereby awarded to (Respondent/ Petitioner/ other).

Note: If custody is awarded to Petitioner and Respondent, jointly, then leave out the reference to visitation. If visitation is to be ordered for specific times and places, put that here and omit the word "reasonable."

It is further ordered that (Respondent/Petitioner) shall pay to (Petitioner/Respondent/other) the sum of $____ per month per child, as and for child support, payable on the _____ day of each month, beginning (date for first payment after hearing) , 19_, and continuing until said child reaches the age of majority, becomes emancipated, dies, or further order of this court. The total amount to be paid each month for child support is $ ____ .

Optional: It is further ordered that (Respondent/ Petitioner) shall have the right to claim tax exemption for (name of child(ren)) for any year in which support payments for said child are not more than (number) months in arrears.

Note for welfare parents: If the person receiving child support is receiving welfare for the support of minors (AFDC), then child support **must** be paid to an officer of the court. Add these words at the end of the child support order: "Payments are to be made through _____ ." Insert the title of whichever official receives support payments in your county (ask Clerk or social worker). **In Los Angeles County** you are required to get and use a local form, 1287A - Judgment Continuation Sheet (Figure 14a, below). In **any** case, a copy of the Interlocutory Judgment must be personally served on Respondent and proof of service filed. Use a professional as described in Chapter 8d.

Here are two other orders which are occasionally used when there are minors. Adapt them to fit your case, if you use them at all.

> During the term of the support obligation for each child, (Respondent/ Petitioner) shall carry and maintain medical and hospital insurance for the benefit of said child, and/or pay for said child's necessary (medical/ dental expenses) (tuition/ expenses for private school/ trade school/ college so long as child is in attendance at least 3/4 time).
>
> During the term of the child support obligation, (Respondent/ Petitioner) shall carry and maintain a policy of insurance upon his/her life in the amount of $ _____ and shall name as beneficiaries said minor children.

B. SPOUSAL SUPPORT: If none was requested, then no order is necessary, but if spousal support was waived, it is good form to put in the following language:

> Spousal support has been waived by (Petitioner/ Respondent/ Petitioner and Respondent) and the court hereby terminates jurisdiction therein.

If spousal support is to be ordered, use the following:

> It is further ordered that (Respondent/ Petitioner) shall pay to (Petitioner/ Respondent) the sum of $____ per month, as and for spousal support, payable on the ____ day of each month, beginning __(some date after the hearing)__ , 19_, and continuing until death or remarriage of the recipient, or until (some specific date, and/or other condition upon which payments stop), whichever occurs first.

C. PROPERTY AND BILLS:

1. None: If you checked box 4a in the Petition, then you will not need any order regarding property in the Interlocutory Judgment.

2. Divided by agreement: If you checked box 4b in the Petition and have a written Marital Settlement Agreement, then insert one of the following orders into your Interlocutory Judgment. Order **A** is the easy one, but you must use **B** if you are in Los Angeles County. You may run into a judge in some other county who prefers method B, in which case you will have to retype the judgment that way.

A

It is further ordered that the marital settlement agreement of the parties dated _____, 19_, is approved, attached hereto, and incorporated by reference, and each of the parties is ordered to comply with all of the terms and conditions stated therein.

B

The marital settlement agreement of the parties dated (put in date of your agreement), is approved and in accordance therewith the following orders are made:

(Put down any terms of the agreement which are to be carried out after the hearing, such as notice of pension benefits, payment of debts, transfers of property, securing of insurance, etc. You should put the items in the form of an order, using the terms "Petitioner" and "Respondent" to refer to the parties. Refer to the other orders in this section and to your agreement for language to use in phrasing the orders.)

---

3. Divided by the court: If you checked box 4c or 4d on the Petition, insert the following order into your Interlocutory Judgment:

It is further ordered that the community property and obligations of the parties, in order to effectuate a substantially equal division (say "fair division," if you are trying to get an unequal division), is divided as follows: To Petitioner: (list and description as in Petition)
   To Respondent: ditto
   Petitioner is ordered to pay: ditto
   Respondent is ordered to pay: ditto
The parties are ordered to do whatever acts and sign whatever documents may be necessary to carry out these orders.

Note about pension plans: If the community has an interest in a pension plan, it must either be listed in this order and awarded to one of the spouses, or reserved for future decision. There are other ways, but they are not covered here. If you want the court to reserve it for future decision, then add this sentence just before the last sentence in the above order:

> As to the pension plan of (Petitioner/Respondent), (give complete identification, file number, name of employer, etc.) , the court specifically reserves jurisdiction to adjudicate the respective rights of the parties at a future date upon application of either party. (Petitioner/ Respondent) is ordered not to apply for or accept benefits under said plan without prior written notice to (Respondent/ Petitioner) and application to this court for determination and division of community rights in said plan.

Note about property descriptions: Use license numbers of vehicles. If the family home or other real estate is being awarded, it should be listed by its common **and** full legal description, like this: "...the family home at 5841 Trudy Ave., City of Altos, County of Cielo, State of California, more particularly known as (insert here the full legal description, exactly as it appears on your deed)." After the hearing, be sure to file a certified copy of the Interlocutory Judgment with the County Recorder (see Chapter B3d). This makes the court order work as a legal transfer of title to the property.

4. Separate property: If you used Item 5 in the Petition, then insert the following order into your Interlocutory Judgment:

> It is further ordered that the following described property be confirmed as (Petitioner's/Respondent's) separate property: (list)

D. RESTORATION OF WIFE'S FORMER NAME: If the court has been told that the wife wants a former name restored, then check box 4a and enter the former name exactly as she desires it.

Important Note: If the Interlocutory Judgment orders Respondent to pay support or turn over property, the order should be served on Respondent personally by the method described in Chapter 8d. File a Proof of Service (get a form from the Clerk), using Fig. 7 as a guide. This step is **essential** should you ever need to enforce the orders.

Type in the information requested →

If the order is against the Respondent, type "Petitioner" in the 1st blank, and type "Respondent" in the 2nd blank. →

It is further ordered, pursuant to Civil Code Section 4702 (a) that the child support payments ordered shall be made through the office of the Court Trustee and that to each weekly payment of $_____ there shall be added the service charge of 2% as required by law, amounting to $_____, making a total weekly payment of $_____.

It is further ordered that the District Attorney appear on behalf of the Custodial party or the minor child or children for whom the payment has been ordered to enforce this order.

The foregoing child support payment shall be transmitted to the office of the Court Trustee, Post Office Box 3544, Terminal Annex, Los Angeles, California 90051. Payments must be made by check or money order payable to the Court Trustee.

The petitioner's home address is: _____

The respondent's home address is: _____

The employer of the party required to pay support is: _____
and said employer's address is: _____

The social security number of the party required to pay support is: _____.

Each party shall notify the Court Trustee in writing of any change of address in his or her residence or employment within 5 days after any such change.

The attorney for the _____ is directed to cause a copy of this judgment to be personally served upon the _____ and to promptly file a return of service thereof.

(Following orders made if box checked)

☐ It is further ordered, pursuant to Civil Code Section 4380, that the spousal support payments ordered shall be made through the office of the Court Trustee as provided above and that to each weekly payment of $_____, there shall be added the service charge of 2% as required by law, amounting to $_____, making a total weekly payment of $_____.

☐ It is further ordered that the _____ assign his or her wages or salary from employment by _____; his or her employer and such successive employers until further order of Court to the Court Trustee, the sum of $_____ per week, heretofore fixed as child support, payable through the Court Trustee, for the purpose of complying with said support order. This order shall be binding upon the employer upon the service of a copy of this order, and the attorney for _____ is ordered to forthwith serve a copy of this order and wage assignment signed by the employee on said employer. The employer may deduct the sum of One Dollar ($1) for each payment made pursuant to this order. Said payment shall be forwarded by the employer on each pay day of said employee commencing with earnings accruing in the first full payroll period after the date of this order and continuing until further order of Court and shall be transmitted by check or money order payable to the Court Trustee. Said payment shall be forwarded by the employer to the office of the Court Trustee, Post Office Box 3544, Terminal Annex, Los Angeles, California 90051.

☐ Further order as follows:

Dated: _____

_____
Judge of the Superior Court

1287A 761551N-(Rev.2-73)-Cdb 8-73 CONTINUATION SHEET-JUDGMENT (MARRIAGE)

THE
NOTICE OF ENTRY OF JUDGMENT

WHAT IT IS

To become effective, the written order of the court **must** be entered in the Clerk's Judgment Book. To let you know that the entry has been made, and when it was made, the Clerk mails a notice to both parties. You prepare this form for the Clerk, leaving blanks which he fills in.

The first time you use this form is with the Interlocutory Judgment. When it is mailed back to you, take note of the date of entry—it is the date written by the clerk on the first line under the caption. You will need to know this date when you fill out the Request for Final (Chapter 15).

The second time you use this form will be with the Final Judgment.

HOW TO FILL IT OUT

Fill it out as shown in Fig. 15. Prepare the original and make 3 copies.

As indicated above, you will need this form twice, so there are two Notice of Entry forms in the back of this book, one for each time you will need to use it.

Figure 15:
HOW TO FILL OUT THE NOTICE OF ENTRY OF JUDGMENT

type caption as shown in chapter 1

type in your case number

check this box the the first time when used with Interlocutory Judgment.

check this box the second time when used with Final Judgment.

Respondent's name and last known address

Petitioner's name and address

ATTORNEY OR PARTY WITHOUT ATTORNEY (NAME AND ADDRESS)   TELEPHONE NO   FOR COURT USE ONLY

ATTORNEY FOR (NAME)

SUPERIOR COURT OF CALIFORNIA, COUNTY OF
STREET ADDRESS
MAILING ADDRESS
CITY AND ZIP CODE
BRANCH NAME

MARRIAGE OF
PETITIONER

RESPONDENT

NOTICE OF ENTRY OF JUDGMENT   CASE NUMBER

You are notified that the following judgment was entered on (date):

1. ☐ Interlocutory Judgment of Dissolution of Marriage

> THE INTERLOCUTORY JUDGMENT TO WHICH THIS NOTICE REFERS DOES NOT CONSTITUTE A FINAL DISSOLUTION OF MARRIAGE AND THE PARTIES ARE STILL MARRIED. ONE OF THE PARTIES MUST SUBMIT A REQUEST FOR A FINAL JUDGMENT ON THE FORM PRESCRIBED BY RULE 1288. NEITHER PARTY MAY REMARRY UNTIL A FINAL JUDGMENT OF DISSOLUTION IS ENTERED.

2. ☐ Final Judgment of Dissolution of Marriage
3. ☐ Final Judgment of Legal Separation
4. ☐ Final Judgment of Nullity

Dated: . . . .   Clerk, By . . . . , Deputy

CLERK'S CERTIFICATE OF MAILING

I certify that I am not a party to this cause and that a copy of the foregoing was mailed first class, postage prepaid, in a sealed envelope addressed as shown below, and that the mailing of the foregoing and execution of this certificate occurred at (place): . . . . , California,

on (date): . . . .   Clerk, By . . . .   Deputy

Form Adopted by Rule 1290
Judicial Council of California
Revised Effective January 1, 1980   **NOTICE OF ENTRY OF JUDGMENT (FAMILY LAW)**

REQUEST FOR FINAL JUDGMENT

WHAT IT IS

This form tells the court that you want the Final Judgment ordered. You won't be divorced unless and until you request this. This form is filed together with the Final Judgment (Chapter 16), but you must wait until at least 6 months after the service of process and at least two months after entry of the Interlocutory Judgment (see Chapter A10).

Part of this request is your oath that you and your spouse have not become reconciled since the granting of the Interlocutory Judgment. Reconciliation is a state of mind, an intention to live together as man and wife. Simply sleeping together on occasion is not necessarily a reconciliation.

Most counties want a $2 filing fee when you file the last papers.

HOW TO FILL IT OUT

Fill it out as shown in Fig. 16. Prepare the original and make 3 copies.

Note: The court acquired jurisdiction of Respondent on the date that service of process became effective (see text note, Chapter 9). If you used the Appearance & Waiver form, the court acquired jurisdiction on the date that form was filed.

Note: The date of entry of the Interlocutory Judgment which you are to enter at Item 2 is found by looking at the Notice of Entry of Judgment which the Clerk mailed to you after your hearing. It is the date written in by the clerk on the first line under the caption.

Note: If you did **not** request restoration of wife's former name at the hearing, you can do it now: Check box 5 and type in, "Restoration of wife's former name, to wit: (put in full name exactly as she wishes it to be)."

Note: Respondent also has the right to file the last set of papers requesting the Final Judgment.

Figure 16:

HOW TO FILL OUT THE REQUEST FOR FINAL JUDGMENT

type caption as shown in chapter 1

type in your case number

type in same date as Item 2 on Interlocutory Judgment

type in date Interlocutory Judgment was entered. See text note.

See text note on wife's name.

type in name, date and place of signing

your signature

type in "In Pro Per"

ATTORNEY OR PARTY WITHOUT ATTORNEY (NAME AND ADDRESS):

TELEPHONE NO

FOR COURT USE ONLY

ATTORNEY FOR (NAME)

SUPERIOR COURT OF CALIFORNIA, COUNTY OF
STREET ADDRESS
MAILING ADDRESS
CITY AND ZIP CODE
BRANCH NAME

MARRIAGE OF
PETITIONER

RESPONDENT

**REQUEST AND DECLARATION FOR FINAL
JUDGMENT OF DISSOLUTION OF MARRIAGE**

1. The court acquired jurisdiction of the respondent on (date):

2. An Interlocutory Judgment of Dissolution of Marriage was entered on (date):

3. Since entry of the Interlocutory Judgment the parties have not become reconciled and have not agreed to dismiss this proceeding. No motion or other proceeding to set aside or annul, and no appeal from that part of the interlocutory judgment granting dissolution of the marriage, is pending and undetermined, and that part of the judgment has become final.

4. I request that final judgment of dissolution of marriage be entered.
   a. ☐ Endorsed copies of a Joint Petition for Summary Dissolution and a Notice of Revocation are attached and I request entry of final judgment pursuant to Civil Code section 4514(b).
   b. ☐ I request judgment be entered effective (nunc pro tunc)
      (1) As of (date):
      (2) For the following reason:

5. ☐ Other request (specify):

6. I declare under penalty of perjury that the foregoing is true and correct and that this declaration is executed on (date): . . . . at (place): . . . . , California.

. . . .
(Type or print name)   (Signature of declarant)

. . . .
(Type or print name)   (Signature of attorney for declarant)

The declaration under penalty of perjury must be signed in California, or in a state that authorizes use of a declaration in place of an affidavit; otherwise an affidavit is required.

Form Adopted by Rule 1288
Judicial Council of California
Revised Effective January 1, 1980

**REQUEST AND DECLARATION FOR FINAL
JUDGMENT OF DISSOLUTION OF MARRIAGE
(FAMILY LAW)**

CC 4514, 4515

THE FINAL JUDGMENT

WHAT IT IS

This is the one you've been waiting for! This is the order of the court declaring that your marriage is over, and restoring you to the status of a single person. It automatically incorporates all of the terms of the Interlocutory Judgment, so the orders don't have to be rewritten here again. It is effective as soon as it is signed by the judge **and** entered in the Judgment Book by the clerk.

Don't forget to file the Notice of Entry of Judgment form with this Final (see Chapter 14).

HOW TO FILL IT OUT

Fill it out as shown in Fig. 17. Prepare the original and make 3 copies.

Note: The court acquired jurisdiction of Respondent on the date that service of process became effective (see text notes, Chapter 9) or, if you used the Appearance & Waiver form, on the date that form was filed.

Note: If restoration of wife's former name was requested on your Request for Final form, then check box 3b and type in the name exactly as she wishes it to be.

Figure 17:

HOW TO FILL OUT THE FINAL JUDGMENT

type in caption as shown in chapter 1

check this box

type in same date as Item 2 on Interlocutory Judgment

check this box

see text note

type in your case number

ATTORNEY OR PARTY WITHOUT ATTORNEY (NAME AND ADDRESS):		TELEPHONE NO.	FOR COURT USE ONLY
ATTORNEY FOR (NAME)			

SUPERIOR COURT OF CALIFORNIA, COUNTY OF
STREET ADDRESS
MAILING ADDRESS
CITY AND ZIP CODE
BRANCH NAME

MARRIAGE OF
PETITIONER

RESPONDENT

FINAL JUDGMENT OF	☑ **DISSOLUTION OF MARRIAGE** ☐ **LEGAL SEPARATION** ☐ **NULLITY**	CASE NUMBER:

1. The court acquired jurisdiction of the respondent on (date):

2. THE COURT ORDERS

   a. ☐ A final judgment of dissolution be entered, and the parties are restored to the status of unmarried persons.
   b. ☐ A judgment of legal separation be entered.
   c. ☐ A judgment of nullity be entered on the ground of (specify):

      and the parties are declared to be unmarried persons.

3. ☐ THE COURT FURTHER ORDERS

   a. ☐ This judgment be entered nunc pro tunc as of (date):
   b. ☐ Wife's former name be restored (specify):
   c. ☐ Other:

Dated: _____   _____
                                    Judge of the Superior Court

☐ Signature follows last attachment.

4. Total number of pages attached:

No attachment permitted on less than a full page. Cal Rules of Ct 201(b)

Form Adopted by Rule 1289
Judicial Council of California
Revised January 1, 1980

**FINAL JUDGMENT
(FAMILY LAW)**

CC 4514, 4515

APPENDIX TO PART TWO

A. Appearance & Waivers

To put it simply, if the Appearance and Waivers (A&W) form is filed, it is a legal appearance by Respondent telling the court that it can render a judgment in his absence without further notice to him. This procedure has advantages over serving papers on your spouse (Chapter 8) because you do not have to serve papers, wait thirty days, or file a Request for Default form. If box 5 is checked, you can also avoid the 60 day appeal period after your hearing (Chapter A10). If Respondent is on **active** military duty, you can **only** proceed by filing a military waiver, which is nicely accomplished with this A&W form. Even if Respondent is not in the military, this is a very convenient procedure to use. However, be aware that a response filing fee of about $70 will be charged **unless** Respondent is in the military, in which case the fee will be waived according to the provisions of Gov. Code 26857.5.

HOW TO DO IT

1. File the first papers as shown in Chapter 3, Step One.

2. Fill out the A&W form as shown in Fig. 18. Prepare the original and 2 copies.

3. Send all copies to Respondent, together with copies of the first papers. Tell Respondent to date and sign two A&W forms, just as the name appears in the caption, then return the original and one signed copy to you. Respondent keeps a copy of the form and the copies of the first papers, but has no further responsibility in the case. If you wish, you can make a written agreement part of this stipulation, or it can be done at a later time.

4. File the completed A&W form as soon as you get it back from Respondent, along with the **original** Summons, left blank on the back. If required in your case (see Chapter 11) also file the Income and Expense and/or the Property Declaration at this time.

5. As soon as you file these papers, you may request a date for your hearing (Chapter 12).

6. Proceed with Steps 5 and 6 just as shown in Chapter 3.

7. The court acquires jurisdiction on the date the A&W form is filed. This date commences the six month waiting period described in Chapter A10.

A copy of the Appearance and Waiver form is provided with this book.

Figure 18: APPEARANCE, STIPULATIONS, & WAIVERS

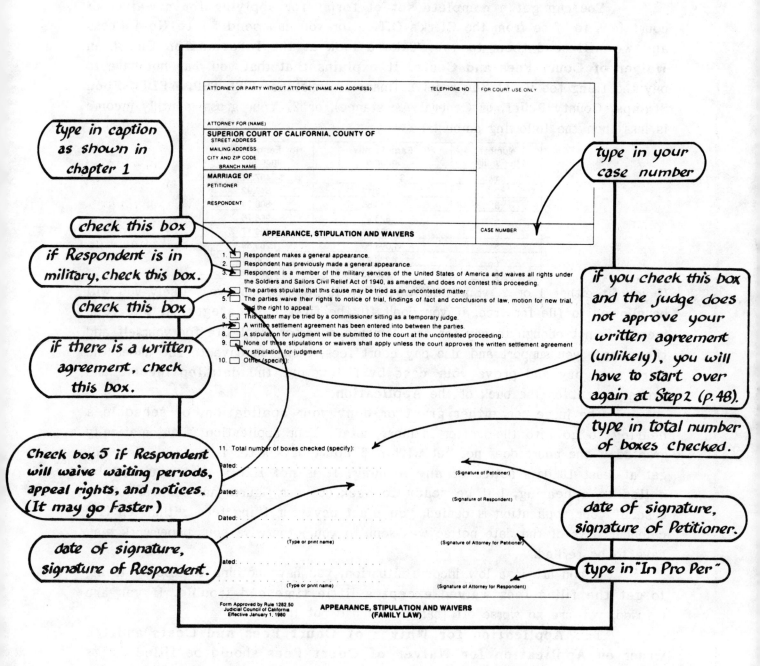

type in caption as shown in chapter 1

type in your case number

check this box

if Respondent is in military, check this box.

check this box

if there is a written agreement, check this box.

if you check this box and the judge does not approve your written agreement (unlikely), you will have to start over again at Step 2 (p. 48).

type in total number of boxes checked.

Check box 5 if Respondent will waive waiting periods, appeal rights, and notices. (It may go faster.)

date of signature, signature of Petitioner.

date of signature, signature of Respondent.

type in "In Pro Per"

Form content:

ATTORNEY OR PARTY WITHOUT ATTORNEY (NAME AND ADDRESS): TELEPHONE NO   FOR COURT USE ONLY

ATTORNEY FOR (NAME)

SUPERIOR COURT OF CALIFORNIA, COUNTY OF
STREET ADDRESS
MAILING ADDRESS
CITY AND ZIP CODE
BRANCH NAME

MARRIAGE OF
PETITIONER

RESPONDENT

APPEARANCE, STIPULATION AND WAIVERS   CASE NUMBER

1. ☐ Respondent makes a general appearance.
2. ☐ Respondent has previously made a general appearance.
3. ☐ Respondent is a member of the military services of the United States of America and waives all rights under the Soldiers and Sailors Civil Relief Act of 1940, as amended, and does not contest this proceeding.
4. ☐ The parties stipulate that this cause may be tried as an uncontested matter.
5. ☐ The parties waive their rights to notice of trial, findings of fact and conclusions of law, motion for new trial, and the right to appeal.
6. ☐ This matter may be tried by a commissioner sitting as a temporary judge.
7. ☐ A written settlement agreement has been entered into between the parties.
8. ☐ A stipulation for judgment will be submitted to the court at the uncontested proceeding.
9. ☐ None of these stipulations or waivers shall apply unless the court approves the written settlement agreement or stipulation for judgment.
10. ☐ Other (specify):

11. Total number of boxes checked (specify):

Dated: ....
                                                        (Signature of Petitioner)

Dated: ....
                                                        (Signature of Respondent)

Dated: ....

....
(Type or print name)   (Signature of Attorney for Petitioner)

Dated: ....

....
(Type or print name)   (Signature of Attorney for Respondent)

Form Approved by Rule 1282.50
Judicial Council of California
Effective January 1, 1980
**APPEARANCE, STIPULATION AND WAIVERS
(FAMILY LAW)**

B. Pauper's Oath

If you are **very** poor, you may not have to pay the filing fees. You don't have to be absolutely destitute, but not too far from it, either. They won't give up the filing fees just because it is inconvenient for you to pay.

You can get a complete set of forms for applying for a waiver of court fees for free from the Clerk's Office, or you can send $3 to Nolo Press and we will send them to you. Take a look at the **Information Sheet on Waiver of Court Fees and Costs.** It explains that that you may not have to pay the filing fee if: **1)** You receive financial assistance (SSI, SSP, AFDC, Food Stamps, County Relief, or General Assistance), or **2)** Your gross monthly income is less then the following amounts:

Number In Family	Farm Family Income	Non-Farm Family Income
1	$ 417.71	$ 487.51
2	553.13	647.92
3	688.55	808.34
4	823.96	968.76
5	959.38	1,129.17
6	1,094.80	1,289.59
7	1,230.21	1,450.01
8	1,365.63	1,610.42

If you fit either 1 or 2, your application will be easy and very likely you will be allowed to file for free. If you don't fit the first two categories, but your income is not enough to pay for the common necessaries of life for yourself and the people you support and also pay court fees, then you have to file under the third category and prove your case by filling out the detailed income and expense sheet on the back of the **Application.**

The judge can either grant or deny your application, or schedule a hearing to go into the matter in more detail. Your application is automatically granted if the court does not act within 5 court days after it is filed. You will get at least 10 days notice of any hearing. It is not likely that you will be called to a hearing, but be ready to back up your figures and claims, just in case. If your application is denied, you **must** pay your filing fees within ten (10) calendar days of the date notice was sent to you, otherwise your paperwork may have to be refiled.

If you are in a low income situation, you have nothing to lose by trying to get the filing fees waived except a little time and trouble. If you are refused, you are no worse off than if you had not tried.

The **Application for Waiver of Court Fees and Costs** and the **Order on Application for Waiver of Court Fees** should be filled out as shown in Figures 19 through 22. They are filed together with your first papers (Chapter 3, Step One). Prepare the originals and make two copies of each.

Figure 19: **APPLICATION FOR WAIVER OF FEES (front)**

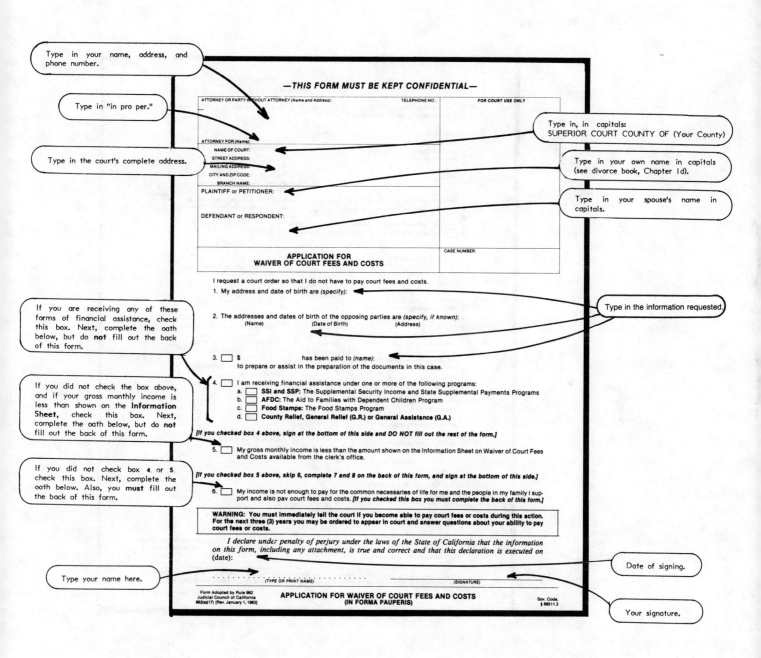

Type in your name, address, and phone number.

Type in "in pro per."

Type in the court's complete address.

Type in, in capitals:
SUPERIOR COURT COUNTY OF (Your County)

Type in your own name in capitals (see divorce book, Chapter 1d).

Type in your spouse's name in capitals.

If you are receiving any of these forms of financial assistance, check this box. Next, complete the oath below, but do **not** fill out the back of this form.

If you did not check the box above, and if your gross monthly income is less than shown on the **Information Sheet,** check this box. Next, complete the oath below, but do **not** fill out the back of this form.

If you did not check box 4. or 5. check this box. Next, complete the oath below. Also, you **must** fill out the back of this form.

Type in the information requested.

Type your name here.

Date of signing.

Your signature.

—THIS FORM MUST BE KEPT CONFIDENTIAL—

ATTORNEY OR PARTY WITHOUT ATTORNEY *(Name and Address)*:   TELEPHONE NO.:   FOR COURT USE ONLY

ATTORNEY FOR *(Name)*:
NAME OF COURT:
STREET ADDRESS:
MAILING ADDRESS:
CITY AND ZIP CODE:
BRANCH NAME:
PLAINTIFF or PETITIONER:

DEFENDANT or RESPONDENT:

**APPLICATION FOR
WAIVER OF COURT FEES AND COSTS**

CASE NUMBER:

I request a court order so that I do not have to pay court fees and costs.

1. My address and date of birth are *(specify)*:

2. The addresses and dates of birth of the opposing parties are *(specify, if known)*:
   (Name)   (Date of Birth)   (Address)

3. ☐ $ has been paid to *(name)*:
   to prepare or assist in the preparation of the documents in this case.

4. ☐ I am receiving financial assistance under one or more of the following programs:
   a. ☐ **SSI and SSP**: The Supplemental Security Income and State Supplemental Payments Programs
   b. ☐ **AFDC**: The Aid to Families with Dependent Children Program
   c. ☐ **Food Stamps**: The Food Stamps Program
   d. ☐ **County Relief, General Relief (G.R.) or General Assistance (G.A.)**

[If you checked box 4 above, sign at the bottom of this side and DO NOT fill out the rest of the form.]

5. ☐ My gross monthly income is less than the amount shown on the Information Sheet on Waiver of Court Fees and Costs available from the clerk's office.

[If you checked box 5 above, skip 6, complete 7 and 8 on the back of this form, and sign at the bottom of this side.]

6. ☐ My income is not enough to pay for the common necessaries of life for me and the people in my family I support and also pay court fees and costs. *[If you checked this box you must complete the back of this form.]*

WARNING: You must immediately tell the court if you become able to pay court fees or costs during this action. For the next three (3) years you may be ordered to appear in court and answer questions about your ability to pay court fees or costs.

I declare under penalty of perjury under the laws of the State of California that the information on this form, including any attachment, is true and correct and that this declaration is executed on (date):

. . . . *(TYPE OR PRINT NAME)* . . . .   _____
                                                                        (SIGNATURE)

Form Adopted by Rule 982
Judicial Council of California
982(a)(17) [Rev. January 1, 1983]

**APPLICATION FOR WAIVER OF COURT FEES AND COSTS
(IN FORMA PAUPERIS)**

Gov. Code,
§ 68511.3

FINANCIAL INFORMATION

7. ☐ My pay changes considerably from month to month. *[If you check this box, each of the amounts reported in 8 should be your average for the past 12 months.]*

8. My monthly income:

   a. My gross monthly pay is: . . . .$_____

   b. My payroll deductions are *(specify purpose and amount)*:

      (1) _____ $_____
      (2) _____ $_____
      (3) _____ $_____
      (4) _____ $_____

      My TOTAL payroll deduction amount is:.$_____

   c. My monthly take-home pay is *(a minus b)*:$_____

   d. Other money I get each month is *(specify source and amount)*:

      (1) _____ $_____
      (2) _____ $_____

      The TOTAL amount of other money is: . .$_____

   e. **MY TOTAL MONTHLY INCOME IS** *(c plus d)*: . . . .$_____

   f. The number of people in my family, including me, supported by this money is: _____

9. a. ☐ I am **not** able to pay any of the court fees and costs.

   b. ☐ I am able to pay **only** the following court fees and costs *(specify)*:

   > Check this box.

10. My monthly expenses are:

   a. Rent or house payment & maintenance .$_____
   b. Food and household supplies . . . .$_____
   c. Utilities and telephone . . . .$_____
   d. Clothing . . . .$_____
   e. Laundry and cleaning . . . .$_____
   f. Medical and dental payments . . . .$_____
   g. Insurance (life, health, accident, etc.) . . .$_____
   h. School, child care . . . .$_____
   i. Child, spousal support (prior marriage) .$_____
   j. Transportation and auto expenses (insurance, gas, repair) . . . .$_____
   k. Installment payments *(specify purpose and amount)*:

      (1) _____ $_____
      (2) _____ $_____
      (3) _____ $_____

      The TOTAL amount of monthly installment payments is: . . . .$_____

   l. Amounts deducted due to wage assignments and earnings withholding orders .$_____
   m. Other expenses *(specify)*:

      (1) _____ $_____
      (2) _____ $_____
      (3) _____ $_____
      (4) _____ $_____
      (5) _____ $_____
      (6) _____ $_____

      The TOTAL amount of other monthly expenses is: . . . .$_____

   n. **MY TOTAL MONTHLY EXPENSES ARE** *(add a through m)*: . . . .$_____

11. I own the following property:

   a. Cash . . . .$_____
   b. Checking, savings and credit union accounts *(list banks)*:

      (1) _____ $_____
      (2) _____ $_____
      (3) _____ $_____

   c. Cars, other vehicles and boat equity *(list make, year of each)*:

      (1) _____ $_____
      (2) _____ $_____
      (3) _____ $_____

   d. Real estate equity . . . .$_____

   e. Other personal property—jewelry, furniture, furs, stocks, bonds, etc. *(list separately)*:

      $_____

12. Other facts which support this application are *(describe unusual medical needs, expenses for recent family emergencies, or other unusual expenses to help the judge understand your budget)*. If more space is needed, attach page labeled attachment 12.

> **WARNING:** You must immediately tell the court if you become able to pay court fees or costs during this action. For the next three (3) years you may be ordered to appear in court and answer questions about your ability to pay court fees or costs.

Figure 21: ORDER FOR WAIVER OF FEES (front)

Fill out the caption as shown for the **Application for Waiver of Court Fees and Costs.**

The rest of this side is filled out by the Clerk and the Judge. Your name and address goes on the back side.

ATTORNEY OR PARTY WITHOUT ATTORNEY (Name and Address):	TELEPHONE NO.:	FOR COURT USE ONLY

ATTORNEY FOR (Name):
NAME OF COURT AND BRANCH, IF ANY:
STREET ADDRESS
MAILING ADDRESS
CITY, ZIP CODE
PLAINTIFF:

DEFENDANT:

ORDER ON APPLICATION FOR WAIVER OF COURT FEES AND COSTS

CASE NUMBER:

1. The application was filed
   a. on (date):
   b. by (name):

2. ☐ **IT IS ORDERED** that the application is granted and the applicant is permitted to proceed in this action as **follows:**
   a. ☐ without payment of any court fees or costs listed in rule 985(i), California Rules of Court.
   b. ☐ without payment of any court fees or costs listed in rule 985(i), California Rules of Court, except the following:

   c. ☐ without payment of the following court fees or costs (specify):

   d. The reasons for denial of any requested waiver are (specify):

   e. The clerk of the court is directed to mail a copy of this order to the applicant only.

3. ☐ **IT IS ORDERED** that the application is denied for the following reasons (specify):

   a. The applicant must pay any fees and costs due in this action within ten days from the date of service of this order or any paper filed by the applicant with the clerk will be of no effect.
   b. The clerk of the court is directed to mail a copy of this order to all parties who have appeared in this action.

4. ☐ **IT IS ORDERED** that a hearing be held.
   a. The substantial evidentiary conflict to be resolved by the hearing is (specify):

   b. Applicant should be present at the hearing to be held (specify):

hearing date:	time:	in ☐ Dept.:	☐ Div.:	☐ Rm.:
address of court:				

   c. The clerk of the court is directed to mail a copy of this order to the applicant only.

Dated: . . . .

(Clerk's certification on page 2)

(Signature of Judge)

Form Adopted by Rule 982
Judicial Council of California
Effective January 1, 1981

ORDER OF APPLICATION FOR WAIVER OF COURT FEES AND COSTS (IN FORMA PAUPERIS)

Govt. Code
§ 68511 3

Figure 22: **ORDER FOR WAIVER OF FEES (back)**

Type your name in capitals.

Type your spouse's name in capitals.

Type your name and complete address.

PLAINTIFF (Name):

DEFENDANT (Name):

CASE NUMBER:

ORDER ON APPLICATION FOR WAIVER OF COURT FEES AND COSTS   Page 2

CLERK'S CERTIFICATE OF MAILING

I certify that I am not a party to this cause and that a copy of the foregoing was mailed first class, postage prepaid, in a sealed envelope addressed as shown below, and that the mailing of the foregoing and execution of this certificate occurred at (place): . . . . , California,

on (date): . . . . , Clerk, by _____
(Deputy)

CLERK'S CERTIFICATION

(SEAL)

I certify that the forgoing is a true copy of the original on file in my office.

Dated: . . . . Clerk, by . . . .
(Deputy)

C. How to Avoid the Hearing

In Regular Dissolution cases, you **may** be able to avoid the court appearance by filing a sworn statement to take the place of your testimony. This is called a **Declaration for Default or Uncontested Dissolution.** In general, it works very nicely. However, some people find it almost as much trouble as just going to the hearing. If there are to be support orders, some judges require that **both** parties file the Income and Expense Declaration, which isn't always possible. What's worse, some judges won't accept them at all, so you end up going to a hearing anyway. But apart from the extra trouble, you have nothing to lose by trying.

Even judges who don't normally admit these affidavits are more likely to accept them if you can also swear that there is some important and compelling reason which keeps you from personally appearing in court. Typical grounds for not being able to come to a hearing might be: sickness, moved out of state and can't afford the trip back, can't get time off from work or caring for handicapped relative, and so on. If you have some compelling reason for not attending the hearing, type an additional title on the front, "AND DECLARATION OF UNAVAILABILITY," as shown in Figure 23. Then in the place shown in the illustrations, type in, "I am unable to attend a hearing because...," and state the reason.

HOW TO DO IT

Fill out the form as shown in Figures 23 and 24. Prepare the original and make two copies. Read the form carefully and check the boxes which apply to your own case, and which refer to the various orders in your Interlocutory Judgment. You can get this form for free from your Clerk, or by sending $2 to **Nolo Press.** In L.A. County you also need to get local form 187 from the Clerk.

You can file the affidavit at the same time as the Request for Entry of Default (Chapter 3, Step 3) or any time thereafter. However, whenever you file the affidavit you **must** also file with it the papers listed in Ch.3, Step 5.

If all goes well, you will get the signed Interlocutory Judgment back in the mail. If not, you will just have to pick up at Step 4 and request a hearing.

Figure 23: DECLARATION FOR UNCONTESTED DISSOLUTION
(front)

Type in Caption as shown in Chapter 1

type in your case number

If applicable, type in "AND DECLARATION OF UNAVAILABILITY" here.

check this box

Read carefully and check boxes relevant to your own case.

ATTORNEY OR PARTY WITHOUT ATTORNEY (NAME AND ADDRESS):　　TELEPHONE:　　FOR COURT USE ONLY

ATTORNEY FOR (NAME):

SUPERIOR COURT OF CALIFORNIA, COUNTY OF
STREET ADDRESS
MAILING ADDRESS
CITY AND ZIP CODE
BRANCH NAME

MARRIAGE OF
PETITIONER:

RESPONDENT:

**DECLARATION FOR DEFAULT
OR UNCONTESTED DISSOLUTION**　　CASE NUMBER:

1. I declare that if I appeared in court and were sworn, I would testify to the truth of the facts in this declaration.

2. I stipulate that proof will be by this declaration and that I will not appear before the court unless I am ordered by the court to do so.

3. Either the petitioner or the respondent has been a resident of this county for at least three months and of the State of California for at least six months continuously and immediately preceding the date of the filing of the Petition for Dissolution of Marriage in this action.

4. All the information in the ☐ petition ☐ response is true and correct.

5. The default of the respondent was entered in these proceedings **OR** the parties have stipulated that the matter may proceed as an uncontested matter without notice.

6. There are irreconcilable differences that have led to the irremediable breakdown of the marriage and there is no possibility of saving the marriage through counseling or other means.

7. This declaration may be reviewed by a commissioner sitting as a temporary judge and that judge may determine whether to grant this request or require my appearance under section 4511 of the Civil Code.

8. PROPERTY AGREEMENT—Check a. or b.
   a. ☐ The parties have entered into an agreement regarding their property and marital rights, the original or a true copy of which is or has been submitted, and the court is requested to approve the agreement.
   OR
   b. ☐ There is **NO AGREEMENT**, and the following statements are true: *(check at least one)*
      (1) ☐ There are no community or quasi-community assets to be disposed of by the court.
      (2) ☐ There are no community debts to be disposed of by the court.
      (3) ☐ The division of community and quasi-community assets and debts is set forth in the proposed Interlocutory Judgment of Dissolution of Marriage. It constitutes a fair and equal division of the property and debts.

(Continued)

Form Approved by Rule 1286.5
Judicial Council of California
Effective January 1, 1982

**DECLARATION FOR DEFAULT
OR UNCONTESTED DISSOLUTION
(FAMILY LAW)**

Civil Code section 4511
CRC Rule 1241

Figure 24: **DECLARATION FOR UNCONTESTED DISSOLUTION**
(back)

Type in names of parties, i.e. "SMITH, JOHN & MARY"

type in your case number

MARRIAGE OF (last name—first name of parties):   CASE NUMBER:

DECLARATION FOR DEFAULT OR UNCONTESTED DISSOLUTION (FAMILY LAW)   Page two

9. SUPPORT *If a support order or attorney fees are requested, submit a completed Judicial Council form 1285.50, Income and Expense Declaration, unless a current form is on file. Include your best estimate of the other party's income and expenses.*

   a. **Spousal Support** *(check one)*
     (1) ☐ I knowingly give up forever any right to receive spousal support.
     (2) ☐ I ask the court to reserve jurisdiction to award spousal support in the future.
     (3) ☐ Spousal support should be ordered as set forth in the proposed Interlocutory Judgment of Dissolution.

   b. ☐ **Child Support** should be ordered as set forth in the proposed Interlocutory Judgment of Dissolution of Marriage.

   c. ☐ **Attorney Fees** should be ordered as set forth in the proposed Interlocutory Judgment of Dissolution of Marriage.

10. ☐ CHILD CUSTODY should be ordered as set forth in the proposed Interlocutory Judgment of Dissolution of Marriage.

11. ☐ CHILD VISITATION should be ordered as set forth in the proposed Interlocutory Judgment of Dissolution of Marriage.

12. ☐ Petitioner ☐ Respondent is presently receiving public assistance and all support should be made payable to *(specify name and address):*

13. ☐ Wife requests restoration of her former name as set forth in the proposed Interlocutory Judgment of Dissolution of Marriage.

14. ☐ Other:

Read carefully and check boxes relevant to your own case.

15. I ask that the court grant the request for an Interlocutory Judgment of Dissolution of Marriage based upon the foregoing grounds and that the court grant the orders set forth in the proposed interlocutory judgment.

I declare under penalty of perjury under the laws of the State of California that the foregoing is true and correct and that this declaration is executed on

(date): *type in date*

your name
(Type or print name)

your signature
(Signature)

Page two

If applicable, this is where you can type in the reason for your unavailability. See text.

APPENDIX TO PART TWO   127

D. Publication of Summons

If your spouse cannot be located, it is still possible to get your divorce. However, a special method of service must be used, called Service by Publication. Although it is a lot of bother, it is not all that difficult.

When you file your Application for Order of Publication, you must be able to prove to the court that you have exhausted all other means to locate and serve Respondent. You should do all of the following steps. Keep copies of your letters and responses, and keep a diary of contacts.

1. Try personal service (Chapter 8d). Use the Sheriff or a professional, as they can give you documentation of their inability to find your spouse.

2. Try service by mail (Chapters 8e and 8f). Be sure to label the envelope "Return in 5 days if undeliverable." Send it registered and keep returns to show failure.

3. Contact all relatives and friends who might know Respondent's whereabouts.

4. Contact Respondent's last known employer.

5. Contact the Dept. of Motor Vehicles for last known address (and attempt service if address is more recent than the one you've had).

6. If you are on welfare, contact the District Attorney's Office to seek aid in locating Respondent.

7. Contact the County Tax Assessor.

8. Contact the Registrar of Voters.

If all this turns up nothing, you then petition the court for permission to publicize by filling out the two forms as shown in Figs. 25-28. These forms are available at your clerk's office or for $4 from **Nolo Press**, Box 544, Occidental, CA. 95465. Contact the Clerk's Office to find out what local newspapers they use for publication. Call around to ask how much publication will cost. File the forms (original and 2 copies) and when the judge signs your order, take the papers to the newspaper office. The paper will publish the summons once a week for four weeks, then mail confirmation of publication to you.

Fill out the Proof of Service as shown in Fig.24 and attach the confirmation of publication. The effective date of service is seven days after the last date of publication. Wait 30 days after that, then file your Proof of Service along with the rest of the second set of papers (see Chapter 3) and proceed as shown in the rest of the book.

Figure 25: **APPLICATION FOR ORDER OF PUBLICATION (front)**

type into blanks as shown below...

type caption as shown in chapter 1

Name, Address and Telephone Number of Attorney(s)

Space Below for Use of Court Clerk Only

Attorney(s) for ....

SUPERIOR COURT OF CALIFORNIA, COUNTY OF

(Title of Action)

Case Number ....

type in your case number

APPLICATION FOR ORDER FOR PUBLICATION
OF **Summons (marriage)**

(Insert word Summons or Citation or name of the summons outstanding—i.e., on Amended Complaint, on Complaint and amendment thereto, etc.)

Application is hereby made for an order directing service of the above captioned summons or citation on defendant, respondent, or citee **(Respondent's name)** by publication of said summons or citation in the **(name of newspaper)** , which newspaper is adjudicated a newspaper of general circulation in California and most likely to give notice to defendant, respondent or citee because **respondent is most likely to read said summons in said newspaper.**

The **marriage** complaint or petition, which is for **dissolution of marriage** was filed herein on **(date of filing petition)**

A copy of the summons or citation and the complaint or petition could not be served by the following methods for the reasons shown:

1. Handing copies to the person to be served. (Personal service ¶415.10 CCP).

2. Leaving during usual office hours copies in the office of the person to be served with the person who apparently was in charge and by thereafter mailing copies (by first class mail, postage prepaid) to the person to be served at the place where the copies were left. (Service on a corporation, partnership, association, or public entity ¶415.20(a) CCP).

3. Leaving copies at the dwelling house, usual place of abode, or usual place of business of the person to be served in the presence of a competent member of the household or a person apparently in charge of his office or place of business, at least 18 years of age, who shall be informed of the general nature of the papers and by thereafter mailing copies (by first class mail, postage prepaid) to the person to be served at the place where the copies were left. (Service on natural person, minor, incompetent, or candidate ¶415.20(b) CCP).

4. Sending (by first class mail or airmail) copies to the person to be served, together with two copies of required form of notice and acknowledgment and a return envelope, postage prepaid, addressed to the sender. (Service by mail ¶415.30 CCP).

5. Sending (by registered or certified airmail with return receipt requested) copies to the person to be served. (Service by mail outside the State of California ¶415.40 CCP).

6. Any other method (Other ¶413.10, 413.30).

(Continued on Reverse)

APPLICATION FOR ORDER
FOR PUBLICATION

Figure 26: **APPLICATION FOR ORDER OF PUBLICATION (back)**

If the service could not be made because the dwelling house, normal place of abode, or the usual place of business of the defendant is unknown, state below the efforts made to determine these locations. If necessary attach declarations of search, declarations by investigators, etc., to this declaration:

(List and describe all efforts to locate and serve Respondent. Attach documentation.)

Executed (date of signing), at (place signed), California.

I declare under penalty of perjury that the foregoing is true and correct.

(Your signature)

(Signature of Declarant)

IF COMPLAINT OR PETITION IS NOT VERIFIED, THE DECLARATION OF MERITS BELOW MUST ALSO BE COMPLETED:

(Your name) states: I am the plaintiff or petitioner in the above-mentioned action.

I have fully and fairly stated the facts of said case to Petitioner, in pro per who is ☒ counsel and ~~and I verily him informed that~~ I verily believe that (Respondent's name) is a necessary and proper party

defendant, respondent or citee thereto, and that I have a good cause of action against him as will appear by my marriage

complaint or petition on file herein, which marriage complaint or petition correctly states the cause of action and is incorporated herein by reference as though fully set out.

Executed (date of signing), at (place of signing), California.

I declare under penalty of perjury that the foregoing is true and correct.

(Your signature)

(Signature of Declarant)

Figure 27: **ORDER FOR PUBLICATION**

type caption as shown in chapter 1

Name, Address and Telephone Number of Attorney(s)	Space Below for Use of Court Clerk Only

Attorney(s) for ....

SUPERIOR COURT OF CALIFORNIA, COUNTY OF

In re the marriage of	Case Number *your case #*
Petitioner:	
and	**ORDER FOR PUBLICATION OF SUMMONS (MARRIAGE)**
Respondent:	

Upon reading and filnig evidence consisting of a declaration as provided in Section 415.50 CCP by *(Your name)*
......................................, and it satisfactorily appearing therefrom that the respondent *(Respondent's name)*
cannot be served with reasonable diligence in any other manner specified in article 3, Chapter 4, Title 5 of the Code of Civil Procedure, and it also appearing from the verified petition that a good cause of action exists in this action in favor of the petitioner therein and against the respondent and that the said respondent is a necessary and proper party to the action or that the party to be served has or claims an interest in real or personal property in this state that is subject to the jurisdiction of the Court or the relief demanded in the

action consists wholly or in part in excluding such party from any interest in such property: NOW, on motion of *Petitioner,*
in pro per ...., Attorney(s) for the Petitioner(s), IT IS ORDERED that the service of said summons in this action be made upon said respondent by publication thereof in the *name of paper* ...., a newspaper of general circulation, published in *city* .... California, hereby designated as the newspaper most likely to give notice to said respondent; that said publication be made at least once a week for four successive weeks.

IT IS FURTHER ORDERED that a copy of said summons and of said petition in this action and, if the petition be for dissolution or for legal separaton, a blank copy of the Confidential Questionnaire (Marriage), be forthwith deposited in the United States Post Office, postpaid, directed to said respondent **if his address is ascertained before expiration of the time prescribed for the publication of this summons or citation and a declaration of this mailing or of the fact that the address was not ascertained be filed at the expiration of the time prescribed for the publication.**

Dated...

....
Judge of the Superior Court

**ORDER FOR PUBLICATION OF
SUMMONS (MARRIAGE)**

Figure 28: **PROOF OF SERVICE (back of summons)**

PROOF OF SERVICE
(Use separate proof of service for each person served)

1. I served the Summons (Family Law) and Petition (Family Law) on respondent (name): *Respondent's name*

   a. with (1) ☐ blank Confidential Counseling Statement   (5) ☐ completed and blank Property Declarations
         (2) ☐ Order to Show Cause and Application   (6) ☐ Other (specify):
         (3) ☐ blank Responsive Declaration
         (4) ☐ completed and blank Income and
            Expense Declarations

   b. ☐ By leaving copies with (name and title or relationship to person served):

   c. ☐ By delivery at ☐ home ☐ business
         (1) Date of: (3) Address:
         (2) Time of:

   d. ☐ By mailing
         (1) Date of: (2) Place of:

2. Manner of service. (Check proper box)

   a. ☐ **Personal service.** By personally delivering copies to the person served. (CCP 415.10)

   b. ☐ **Substituted service on natural person, minor, incompetent.** By leaving copies at the dwelling house, usual place of abode, or usual place of business of the person served in the presence of a competent member of the household or a person apparently in charge of the office or place of business, at least 18 years of age, who was informed of the general nature of the papers, and thereafter mailing (by first-class mail, postage prepaid) copies to the person served at the place where the copies were left. (CCP 415.20(b)) **(Attach separate declaration or affidavit stating acts relied on to establish reasonable diligence in first attempting personal service.)**

   c. ☐ **Mail and acknowledgment service.** By mailing (by first-class mail or airmail) copies to the person served, together with two copies of the form of notice and acknowledgment and a return envelope, postage prepaid, addressed to the sender. (CCP 415.30) **(Attach completed acknowledgment of receipt.)**

   d. ☐ **Certified or registered mail service.** By mailing to address outside California (by registered or certified airmail with return receipt requested) copies to the person served. (CCP 415.40) **(Attach signed return receipt or other evidence of actual delivery to the person served.)**

   e. ☒ Other (Specify code section): *CCP 415·5*
         ☐ Additional page is attached.

3. The notice to the person served (Item 2 on the copy of the summons served) was completed as follows (CCP 412.30, 415.10, and 474):

   a. ☒ As an individual

   b. ☐ On behalf of Respondent
         Under: ☐ CCP 416.60 (Minor)   ☐ Other (specify):
                ☐ CCP 416.70 (Ward or Conservatee)
                ☐ CCP 416.90 (Individual)

   c. ☐ By personal delivery on (Date):

4. At the time of service I was at least 18 years of age and not a party to this action.

5. Fee for service: $ *fill in amount*

6. Person serving

   a. ☐ Not a registered California process server.   e. ☐ California sheriff, marshal, or constable.

   b. ☐ Registered California process server.   f. Name, address and telephone number and

   c. ☐ Employee or independent contractor of a   if applicable, county of registration and number:
         registered California process server.

   d. ☐ Exempt from registration under Bus. & Prof.
         Code 22350(b)

   I declare under penalty of perjury that the foregoing   (For California sheriff, marshal or constable use only)
   is true and correct and that this declaration is executed   I certify that the foregoing is true and correct and that
   on (date):   this certificate is executed on (date):
   at (place):   , California.   at (place):   , California.

   ✳ see attached
   (attach papers received from newspaper)

   _____   _____
   (Signature)   (Signature)

   A declaration under penalty of perjury must   signed in California or in a state that authorizes use   declaration in place of an affidavit; otherwise
   an affidavit is required

PART THREE:
HOW TO DO YOUR OWN
SUMMARY DISSOLUTION

THE MAIL ORDER DIVORCE

If you haven't already done so, read Chapter F about the advantages and disadvantages of the Summary Dissolution. You should also read through all of Part One, no matter which procedure you choose.

After several years of experience, it is striking how **little** the Summary Dissolution is being used. We think this is because of the disadvantages pointed out in Chapter F. Please remember our main advice: Don't do it if you think your spouse may file a revocation during the long waiting period, and don't rush into it just to make the deadline. The Regular Dissolution is not that hard to do and it has some advantages over this shorter method.

If you are qualified to use the Summary Dissolution procedure, and if you choose to use it instead of doing a Regular Dissolution, then go to your County Clerk's office and pick up the official **Summary Dissolution Booklet**. It comes with all the forms you need. The law requires **both** you and your spouse to read this booklet before you can file, so you may as well do it now.

The Summary Dissolution booklet is very clear and easy to read, but it too often and too strongly urges you into an attorney's office. We think it is best if you do **not** see a lawyer unless you have a specific question or problem, or if your spouse is raising problems you can't solve on your own. Lawyers cost a lot and have a way of making simple things more complicated.

To file a Summary Dissolution you must follow the instructions in the booklet. Unfortunately, the booklet fails to tell you much about filling out the forms, so we have included some instructions and details in the next chapter.

18
HOW TO FILL OUT THE FORMS

Review the Summary Dissolution Booklet. It tells you what forms you need and what to do with them. You will need an original and two copies of any form you file. You can fill out an original and make copies of that, or you can make carbon copies.

Except for the signatures, the forms must be filled in with a typewriter.

18a The Captions

The "captions" are the top part of the forms, and they are all the same. They are filled in like this:

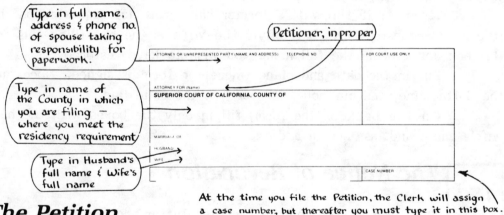

18b The Petition

Item 2: Put down the date of your marriage.

Item 9: Check box (a) if there is **no** community property and **no** community debts. Otherwise you must check box (b) and you must also attach a property settlement agreement to the Petition. See Chapter E2 in this book as well as Chapters IX and X in the Summary Dissolution Booklet.

Item 11: Check this box if Wife wants her former name restored, and type in the full name she desires.

Item 13: Type in the mailing address of Husband and Wife.

The signature of each spouse is required. You should type or write in the date and name of the place where you signed the form. If signed outside California, the oath section must be changed as shown in Chapter 1f.

Take the Petition and two copies to the County Clerk's office, together with the filing fee in cash or money order (call ahead to find out how much money you need). They will stamp the date and case number on the Petition. One copy goes to Husband, one to Wife. Wait at least six months and file the Request for Final Judgment form.

18c The Request for Final Judgment/Notice of Entry

The caption is filled in as shown above. Don't forget to put in the case number stamped on your Petition.

Item 3: Check box (a). Box (b) refers to those rare cases where the final judgment was not properly requested and/or entered at the time you first had a right to it, and for some good reason you need to have it made effective as of the earlier date. For example: If you were told and believed that your spouse entered the final then got married again and later found out your divorce was not entered, you might get the judgment made effective as of the end of the waiting period, **if** the proceeding has not since been revoked or dismissed.

Item 4: If the wife's former name was not requested on the Petition, it can be requested here, but **only**if the wife is the one filing this form. Check this box and type in the full name you wish to have restored.

Put in the date and place where the form is signed, type your name on the dotted line, and put your signature on the solid line.

On the back of the form, fill in only the boxes with the husband's and wife's name and last known address.

18d The Notice of Revocation

This form is used to stop the dissolution. Either spouse can file it. **Do not** file it unless you want the divorce proceeding to be permanently stopped.

The caption is filled out as shown above. Don't forget to put in the case number.

In the first paragraph, put in the date the Petition was filed (the date stamped at the Clerk's office). Then put in the date and place signed, type your name on the dotted line and add your signature on the solid line. If signed outside California, alter the wording as shown in Chapter 1f.

Fill in Husband's and Wife's name and last known address in the boxes provided.

ATTORNEY OR PARTY WITHOUT ATTORNEY (NAME AND ADDRESS):	TELEPHONE NO :	FOR COURT USE ONLY

ATTORNEY FOR (NAME):

SUPERIOR COURT OF CALIFORNIA, COUNTY OF
STREET ADDRESS:

MAILING ADDRESS:

CITY AND ZIP CODE:

BRANCH NAME:

MARRIAGE OF
PETITIONER:

RESPONDENT:

SUMMONS (FAMILY LAW)	CASE NUMBER:

NOTICE!	¡AVISO!
You have been sued. The court may decide against you without your being heard unless you respond within 30 days. Read the information below.	**Usted ha sido demandado. El tribunal puede decidir contra Ud. sin audiencia a menos que Ud. responda dentro de 30 días. Lea la información que sigue.**
If you wish to seek the advice of an attorney in this matter, you should do so promptly so that your response or pleading, if any, may be filed on time.	**Si Usted desea solicitar el consejo de un abogado en este asunto, debería hacerlo inmediatamente, de esta manera, su respuesta o alegación, si hay alguna, puede ser registrada a tiempo.**

1. TO THE RESPONDENT

The petitioner has filed a petition concerning your marriage. If you fail to file a response within 30 days of the date that this summons is served on you, your default may be entered and the court may enter a judgment containing injunctive or other orders concerning division of property, spousal support, child custody, child support, attorney fees, costs, and such other relief as may be granted by the court. The garnishment of wages, taking of money or property, or other court authorized proceedings may also result.

Dated: . . . . Clerk, By _____, Deputy

(SEAL)

2. NOTICE TO THE PERSON SERVED. You are served
   a. ☐ As an individual
   b. ☐ On behalf of Respondent

   Under:
   ☐ CCP 416.60 (Minor)
   ☐ CCP 416.70 (Ward or Conservatee)
   ☐ CCP 416.90 (Individual)
   ☐ Other (specify):

   c. ☐ By personal delivery on (Date):

(See reverse for Proof of Service)

The response (printed form rule 1282) and other permitted papers must be in the form prescribed by the California Rules of Court. They must be filed in this court with the proper filing fee and proof of service of a copy of each on petitioner. The time when the 30 days to respond begins may vary depending on the method of service. For example, see CCP 413.10-415.50.

Form Adopted by Rule 1283 Judicial Council of California Revised Effective January 1, 1980	SUMMONS (FAMILY LAW)	CC 4503 CCP 412.20 CRC 1216

PROOF OF SERVICE

(Use separate proof of service for each person served)

1. I served the Summons (Family Law) and Petition (Family Law) on respondent (name):
   - a. with (1) ☐ blank Confidential Counseling Statement   (5) ☐ completed and blank Property Declarations
     - (2) ☐ Order to Show Cause and Application   (6) ☐ Other (specify):
     - (3) ☐ blank Responsive Declaration
     - (4) ☐ completed and blank Income and Expense Declarations
   - b. ☐ By leaving copies with (name and title or relationship to person served):
   - c. ☐ By delivery at ☐ home ☐ business
     - (1) Date of: (3) Address:
     - (2) Time of:
   - d. ☐ By mailing
     - (1) Date of: (2) Place of:

2. Manner of service: (Check proper box)
   - a. ☐ **Personal service.** By personally delivering copies to the person served. (CCP 415.10)
   - b. ☐ **Substituted service on natural person, minor, incompetent.** By leaving copies at the dwelling house, usual place of abode, or usual place of business of the person served in the presence of a competent member of the household or a person apparently in charge of the office or place of business, at least 18 years of age, who was informed of the general nature of the papers, and thereafter mailing (by first-class mail, postage prepaid) copies to the person served at the place where the copies were left. (CCP 415.20(b)) **(Attach separate declaration or affidavit stating acts relied on to establish reasonable diligence in first attempting personal service.)**
   - c. ☐ **Mail and acknowledgment service.** By mailing (by first-class mail or airmail) copies to the person served, together with two copies of the form of notice and acknowledgment and a return envelope, postage prepaid, addressed to the sender. (CCP 415.30) **(Attach completed acknowledgment of receipt.)**
   - d. ☐ **Certified or registered mail service.** By mailing to address outside California (by registered or certified airmail with return receipt requested) copies to the person served. (CCP 415.40) **(Attach signed return receipt or other evidence of actual delivery to the person served.)**
   - e. ☐ Other (Specify code section):
     - ☐ Additional page is attached.

3. The notice to the person served (Item 2 on the copy of the summons served) was completed as follows (CCP 412.30, 415.10, and 474):
   - a. ☐ As an individual
   - b. ☐ On behalf of Respondent
     - Under: ☐ CCP 416.60 (Minor)   ☐ Other (specify):
       - ☐ CCP 416.70 (Ward or Conservatee)
       - ☐ CCP 416.90 (Individual)
   - c. ☐ By personal delivery on (Date): . . . .

4. At the time of service I was at least 18 years of age and not a party to this action.

5. Fee for service: $ . . . .

6. Person serving
   - a. ☐ Not a registered California process server.   e. ☐ California sheriff, marshal, or constable.
   - b. ☐ Registered California process server.   f. Name, address and telephone number and
   - c. ☐ Employee or independent contractor of a registered California process server.   if applicable, county of registration and number:
   - d. ☐ Exempt from registration under Bus. & Prof. Code 22350(b)

I declare under penalty of perjury that the foregoing is true and correct and that this declaration is executed on (date): . . . . at (place): . . . ., California.

(For California sheriff, marshal or constable use only)

I certify that the foregoing is true and correct and that this certificate is executed on (date): . . . . at (place): . . . ., California.

_____
(Signature)

_____
(Signature)

A declaration under penalty of perjury mus_ signed in California or in a state that authorizes use   _eclaration in place of an affidavit; otherwise
an affidavit is required.

ATTORNEY OR PARTY WITHOUT ATTORNEY (Name and Address):	TELEPHONE NO.:	FOR COURT USE ONLY
ATTORNEY FOR (Name):		

SUPERIOR COURT OF CALIFORNIA, COUNTY OF

STREET ADDRESS:

MAILING ADDRESS:

CITY AND ZIP CODE:

BRANCH NAME:

MARRIAGE OF

PETITIONER:

RESPONDENT:

PETITION FOR	CASE NUMBER:
☐ **Dissolution of Marriage** ☐ **And Declaration Under Uniform Child** ☐ **Legal Separation** **Custody Jurisdiction Act** ☐ **Nullity of Marriage**	

1. RESIDENCE (Dissolution only) ☐ Petitioner ☐ Respondent has been a resident of this state for at least six months and of this county for at least three months immediately preceding the filing of this Petition for Dissolution.

2. STATISTICAL FACTS
   a. Date of marriage:
   b. Date of separation:
   c. Period between marriage and separation
      Years: Months:

3. DECLARATION REGARDING MINOR CHILDREN OF THIS MARRIAGE
   a. ☐ There are no minor children.
   b. ☐ The minor children are:

Name	Birthdate	Age	Sex

   c. IF THERE ARE MINOR CHILDREN, COMPLETE EITHER (1) or (2)
   (1) ☐ Each child named in 3b is presently living with ☐ petitioner ☐ respondent
   at (address):

   and during the last five years has lived in no state other than California and with no person other than petitioner or respondent or both.

   Petitioner has not participated in any capacity in any litigation or proceeding in any state concerning custody of any minor child of this marriage.

   Petitioner has no information of any pending custody proceeding or of any person not a party to this proceeding who has physical custody or claims to have custody or visitation rights concerning any minor child of this marriage.

   (2) ☐ A completed Declaration Under Uniform Custody of Minors Act is attached.

4. ☐ Petitioner requests confirmation of the following as separate assets and obligations:
   Item   Confirm to

(Continued on reverse)

Form Adopted by Rule 1281
Judicial Council of California
1281 [Rev. January 1, 1983]

PETITION
(FAMILY LAW)

MARRIAGE OF (last name—first names of parties):	CASE NUMBER:

5. DECLARATION REGARDING COMMUNITY AND QUASI-COMMUNITY ASSETS AND OBLIGATIONS AS PRESENTLY KNOWN

    a. ☐ There are no such assets or obligations subject to disposition by the court in this proceeding.

    b. ☐ All such assets and obligations have been disposed of by written agreement.

    c. ☐ All such assets and obligations are listed in the property declaration to be filed with this petition.

    d. ☐ All such assets and obligations are listed below:

6. Petitioner requests

    a. ☐ Dissolution of the marriage based on
        (1) ☐ irreconcilable differences. CC 4506(1)
        (2) ☐ incurable insanity. CC 4506(2)

    b. ☐ Legal separation of the parties based on
        (1) ☐ irreconcilable differences. CC 4506(1)
        (2) ☐ incurable insanity. CC 4506(2)

    c. ☐ Nullity of void marriage based on
        (1) ☐ incestuous marriage. CC 4400
        (2) ☐ bigamous marriage. CC 4401

    d. ☐ Nullity of voidable marriage based on
        (1) ☐ petitioner's age at time of marriage. CC 4425(a)
        (2) ☐ prior existing marriage. CC 4425(b)
        (3) ☐ unsound mind. CC 4425(c)
        (4) ☐ fraud. CC 4425(d)
        (5) ☐ force. CC 4425(e)
        (6) ☐ physical incapacity. CC 4425(f)

7. Petitioner requests that the court grant the relief or judgment specified in item 6, make injunctive and other orders as may be proper, and that

    a. ☐ Child custody be awarded
        (1) Legal custody
            (a) ☐ Joint to petitioner and respondent
            (b) ☐ Sole to ☐ petitioner ☐ respondent ☐ other (specify):
        (2) Physical custody
            (a) ☐ Joint to petitioner and respondent
            (b) ☐ Sole to ☐ petitioner ☐ respondent ☐ other (specify):

    b. ☐ Child visitation rights be granted (specify):

    c. ☐ Child support be awarded ☐ petitioner ☐ respondent

    d. ☐ Spousal support be awarded ☐ petitioner ☐ respondent

    e. ☐ Property rights be determined.

    f. ☐ Attorney's fees and costs be awarded ☐ petitioner ☐ respondent

    g. ☐ Wife's former name be restored (specify):

I declare under penalty of perjury under the laws of the State of California that the foregoing is true and correct and that this declaration is executed on
(date):

_____
(SIGNATURE OF PETITIONER)

. . . .
(TYPE OR PRINT NAME OF ATTORNEY)

_____
(SIGNATURE OF ATTORNEY FOR PETITIONER)

Name, Address and Telephone of Attorney(s)

Space Be r Use of Court Clerk Only

Attorney(s) for . . . .

SUPERIOR COURT OF CALIFORNIA, COUNTY OF

In re the marriage of

Petitioner:

and

Respondent:

CASE NUMBER

**DECLARATION UNDER
UNIFORM CUSTODY OF
MINORS ACT**

1. The number of minor children subject to this proceeding is . . . . The name, place of birth, birthdate and sex of each child, the present address, periods of residence and places where each child has lived within the past five (5) years, and the name, present address and relationship to the child of each person with whom the child has lived during that time are: (See footnote *)

Child's Name: A.		Place of Birth	Birthdate:	Sex:
Period of Residence: to present.	Address:		Person Child Lived With: (Name and Present Address)	Relationship:
 to				
 to				
 to				
 to				

Child's Name. B.		Place of Birth:	Birthdate:	Sex:
Period of Residence: to present.	Address:		Person Child Lived With: (Name and Present Address)	Relationship:
 to				
 to				
 to				

Total Number of Continuation Pages Attached . . . . .

* Singular includes plural. Declaration under penalty of perjury must be signed in California (CCP 2015.5) Affidavit is required when signed outside California. When declaration applies to more than two children. attach additional page (CRC 201 (b)).

Form Approved by the
Judicial Council of California
Effective January 1, 1975

DECLARATION UNDER UNIFORM CUSTODY OF MINORS ACT

CC 5158

2. ☐ I have not participated as a party, witness, or in any other capacity in any other litigation or custody proceeding, in this or any other state, concerning custody of a child subject to this proceeding.

☐ I have participated as a party, witness, or in some other capacity in other litigation or custody proceeding, in this or some other state, concerning custody of a child subject to this proceeding, as follows:

   a. Name of each child:

   b. Capacity of declarant:

   c. Court and state:

   d. Date of court order or judgment (if any):

3. ☐ I have no information of any custody proceeding pending in a court of this or any other state concerning a child subject to this proceeding, other than that set out in item 2.

☐ I have the following information concerning a custody proceeding pending in a court of this or some other state concerning a child subject to this proceeding, other than that set out in item 2:

   a. Name of each child:

   b. Nature of proceeding:

   c. Court and state:

   d. Status of proceeding:

4. ☐ I do not know of any person not a party to this proceeding who has physical custody or claims to have custody or visitation rights with respect to any child subject to this proceeding.

☐ I know that the following named person not a party to this proceeding has physical custody or claims custody or visitation rights with respect to a child subject to this proceeding:

   a. Name and address of person: b. Name and address of person: c. Name and address of person:

☐ Has physical custody   ☐ Has physical custody   ☐ Has physical custody
☐ Claims custody rights   ☐ Claims custody rights   ☐ Claims custody rights
☐ Claims visitation rights   ☐ Claims visitation rights   ☐ Claims visitation rights

   a. Name of each child: b. Name of each child: c. Name of each child:

I declare under penalty of perjury that the foregoing, including any attachments, is true and correct and that this declaration is executed on (Date) . . . . at (Place) . . . . ,California.

. . . .   _____

(Type or print name)   (Signature of Declarant)

┌───┐
│ NOTICE TO DECLARANT: You have a continuing duty to inform this court of any information │
│ you obtain of any custody proceeding, in this or in any other state, concerning a child subject │
│ to this proceeding.   │
└───┘

Attorney(s) for . . . .

SUPERIOR COURT OF CALIFORNIA, COUNTY OF . . . .

In re the marriage of

Petitioner:

and

Respondent:

CASE NUMBER

☐ Petitioner's ☐ Respondent's

CONFIDENTIAL COUNSELING STATEMENT
(MARRIAGE)

I understand that conciliation services are available to me through the court in this county.

☐ I would like marriage counseling.

☐ I would like to talk with a trained person about my present family situation.

☐ I do not desire counseling at this time.

Mailing address of requesting party:

Name:

Street:

City/State/Zip

Mailing address of other party:

Name:

Street:

City/State/Zip

Date: _____

_____

(Signature)

ATTORNEY OR PARTY WITHOUT ATTORNEY (NAME AND ADDRESS):	TELEPHONE NO.:	FOR COURT USE ONLY

ATTORNEY FOR (NAME):

SUPERIOR COURT OF CALIFORNIA, COUNTY OF
STREET ADDRESS:
MAILING ADDRESS:
CITY AND ZIP CODE:
BRANCH NAME:

MARRIAGE OF
PETITIONER:

RESPONDENT:

APPEARANCE, STIPULATION AND WAIVERS	CASE NUMBER:

1. ☐ Respondent makes a general appearance.
2. ☐ Respondent has previously made a general appearance.
3. ☐ Respondent is a member of the military services of the United States of America and waives all rights under the Soldiers and Sailors Civil Relief Act of 1940, as amended, and does not contest this proceeding.
4. ☐ The parties stipulate that this cause may be tried as an uncontested matter.
5. ☐ The parties waive their rights to notice of trial, findings of fact and conclusions of law, motion for new trial, and the right to appeal.
6. ☐ This matter may be tried by a commissioner sitting as a temporary judge.
7. ☐ A written settlement agreement has been entered into between the parties.
8. ☐ A stipulation for judgment will be submitted to the court at the uncontested proceeding.
9. ☐ None of these stipulations or waivers shall apply unless the court approves the written settlement agreement or stipulation for judgment.
10. ☐ Other (specify):

11. Total number of boxes checked (specify):

Dated: . . . . _____
(Signature of Petitioner)

Dated: . . . . _____
(Signature of Respondent)

Dated: . . . .

. . . . _____
(Type or print name)   (Signature of Attorney for Petitioner)

Dated: . . . .

. . . . _____
(Type or print name)   (Signature of Attorney for Respondent)

Form Approved by Rule 1282.50
Judicial Council of California
Effective January 1, 1980

**APPEARANCE, STIPULATION AND WAIVERS
(FAMILY LAW)**

NAME AND ADDRESS OF **SENDER**:	TELEPHONE NO.:	For Court Use Only:

SUPERIOR COURT OF CALIFORNIA, COUNTY OF

PLAINTIFF:

DEFENDANT:

NOTICE AND ACKNOWLEDGMENT OF RECEIPT	Case Number:

TO: . . . .
(Insert name of individual being served)

This summons and other document(s) indicated below are being served pursuant to Section 415.30 of the California Code of Civil Procedure. Your failure to complete this form and return it to me within 20 days may subject you (or the party on whose behalf you are being served) to liability for the payment of any expenses incurred in serving a summons on you in any other manner permitted by law.

If you are being served on behalf of a corporation, unincorporated association (including a partnership), or other entity, this form must be signed by you in the name of such entity or by a person authorized to receive service of process on behalf of such entity. In all other cases, this form must be signed by you personally or by a person authorized by you to acknowledge receipt of summons. Section 415.30 provides that this summons and other document(s) are deemed served on the date you sign the Acknowledgment of Receipt below, if you return this form to me.

Dated: . . . .   _____
(Signature of sender)

ACKNOWLEDGMENT OF RECEIPT

This acknowledges receipt of: (To be completed by sender before mailing)
1. ☐ A copy of the summons and of the complaint.
2. ☐ A copy of the summons and of the Petition (Marriage) and:
   ☐ Blank Confidential Counseling Statement (Marriage)
   ☐ Order to Show Cause (Marriage)
   ☐ Blank Responsive Declaration
   ☐ Blank Financial Declaration
   ☐ Other: (Specify)

(To be completed by recipient)

Date of receipt:. . . . .   _____
(Signature of person acknowledging receipt, with title if acknowledgment is made on behalf of another person)

Date this form is signed: . . . .   _____
(Type or print your name and name of entity, if any, on whose behalf this form is signed)

Form Approved by the
Judicial Council of California
Revised Effective January 1, 1975

NOTICE AND ACKNOWLEDGMENT OF RECEIPT

CCP 415.30, 417.10;
Cal. Rules of Court,
Rule 1216

ATTORNEY OR PARTY WITHOUT ATTORNEY (NAME AND ADDRESS):   TELEPHONE NO.:   FOR COURT USE ONLY

ATTORNEY FOR (NAME):

SUPERIOR COURT OF CALIFORNIA, COUNTY OF
  STREET ADDRESS:
  MAILING ADDRESS:
  CITY AND ZIP CODE:
  BRANCH NAME:

MARRIAGE OF
PETITIONER:

RESPONDENT:

| **REQUEST TO ENTER DEFAULT** | CASE NUMBER: |

1. TO THE CLERK: Please enter the default of the respondent who has failed to respond to the petition.
2. A completed ☐ Income and Expense Declaration ☐ Property Declaration is attached.
3. A completed ☐ Income and Expense Declaration ☐ Property Declaration is *not* attached because (check at least one of the following)
    (1) ☐ There have been no changes since the previous filing.
    (2) ☐ The issues subject to disposition by the court in this proceeding are the subject of a written agreement.
    (3) ☐ There are no issues of child custody, child or spousal support, division of community property or attorney fees and costs subject to determination by this court.
    (4) ☐ The petition does not request money, property, costs or attorney fees.

Dated:

. . . .   _____
(Type or print name)   Signature of (Attorney for) Petitioner

3. DECLARATION
    a. ☐ No mailing is required because service was by publication and the address of respondent remains unknown.
    b. ☐ A copy of this Request to Enter Default including any attachments was mailed to the respondent's attorney of record or, if none, to respondent's last known address as follows
        (1) Date of mailing: (2) Addressed as follows:

    c. I declare under penalty of perjury that the foregoing is true and correct and that this declaration is executed on (date): . . . . at (place): . . . ., California.

. . . .   _____
(Type or print name)   (Signature of declarant)

FOR COURT USE ONLY
    Default entered as requested on (date):
                                 Clerk, by:
    Default NOT entered. Reason:

(See reverse for Memorandum of Costs and Declaration of Nonmilitary Status)

The declaration under penalty of perjury must be signed in California or in a state that authorizes use of a declaration in place of an affidavit; otherwise an affidavit is required. (CCP 2015.5)

Form Adopted by Rule 1286
Judicial Council of California
Revised Effective January 1, 1980

REQUEST TO ENTER DEFAULT
(FAMILY LAW)

CCP 585,587

4. MEMORANDUM OF COSTS

  a. ☐ Costs and disbursements are waived.
  b. Costs and disbursements are listed as follows

    (1) ☐ Clerk's fees . . . . $ . . . .

    (2) ☐ Process server's fees . . . . $ . . . .

    (3) ☐ Other (specify) . . . . $ . . . .

    . . . . $ . . . .

    . . . . $ . . . .

    . . . . $ _____

    TOTAL . . . . $ . . . .

I am the attorney, agent, or party who claims these costs. To the best of my knowledge and belief the foregoing items of cost are correct and have been necessarily incurred in this cause or proceeding.

I declare under penalty of perjury that the foregoing is true and correct and that this declaration is executed on (date): . . . . at (place): . . . . , California.

. . . .   _____
        (Type or print name)   (Signature of declarant)

5. DECLARATION OF NONMILITARY STATUS

Respondent is not in the military service or in the military service of the United States as defined in Section 101 of the Soldiers' and Sailors' Relief Act of 1940, as amended, and not entitled to the benefits of such act.

I declare under penalty of perjury that the foregoing is true and correct and that this declaration is executed on (date): . . . . at (place): . . . . , California.

. . . .   _____
        (Type or print name)   (Signature of declarant)

ATTORNEY OR PARTY WITHOUT ATTORNEY (NAME AND ADDRESS):	TELEPHONE NO.:	FOR COURT USE ONLY

ATTORNEY FOR (NAME):

SUPERIOR COURT OF CALIFORNIA, COUNTY OF
STREET ADDRESS:

MAILING ADDRESS:

CITY AND ZIP CODE:

BRANCH NAME:

MARRIAGE OF
PETITIONER:

RESPONDENT:

☐ **PETITIONER'S** ☐ **RESPONDENT'S**

  ☐ **COMMUNITY & QUASI-COMMUNITY PROPERTY DECLARATION**

  ☐ **SEPARATE PROPERTY DECLARATION**

CASE NUMBER:

INSTRUCTIONS

When this form is attached to Petition or Response, values and your proposal regarding division need not be completed. Do not list community, including quasi-community, property with separate property on the same form. Quasi-community property must be so identified. For additional space, use the form "Continuation of Property Declaration."

ITEM NO.	BRIEF DESCRIPTION	GROSS FAIR MARKET VALUE	AMOUNT OF DEBT	NET FAIR MARKET VALUE	PROPOSAL FOR DIVISION AWARD TO PETITIONER	RESPONDENT
		$	$	$	$	$
1.	REAL ESTATE					
2.	HOUSEHOLD FURNITURE, FURNISHINGS, APPLIANCES					
3.	JEWELRY, ANTIQUES, ART, COIN COLLECTIONS, etc.					
4.	VEHICLES, BOATS, TRAILERS					
5.	SAVINGS, CHECKING, CREDIT UNION, CASH					

(Continued on reverse)

The declaration under penalty of perjury must be signed in California or in a state that authorizes use of a declaration in place of an affidavit; otherwise an affidavit is required.

Form Adopted by Rule 1285.55
Judicial Council of California
Effective January 1, 1980

PROPERTY DECLARATION
(FAMILY LAW)

ITEM NO.	BRIEF DESCRIPTION	GROSS FAIR MARKET VALUE	AMOUNT OF DEBT	NET FAIR MARKET VALUE	PROPOSAL FOR DIVISION AWARD TO PETITIONER	RESPONDENT
		$	$	$	$	$
6.	LIFE INSURANCE (CASH VALUE)					
7.	EQUIPMENT, MACHINERY, LIVESTOCK					
8.	STOCKS, BONDS, SECURED NOTES					
9.	RETIREMENT, PENSION, PROFIT-SHARING, ANNUITIES					
10.	ACCOUNTS RECEIVABLE, UNSECURED NOTES, TAX REFUNDS					
11.	PARTNERSHIPS, OTHER BUSINESS INTERESTS					
12.	OTHER ASSETS AND DEBTS					
13.	TOTAL FROM CONTINUATION SHEET					
14.	TOTALS					

15. ☐ A Continuation of Property Declaration is attached and incorporated by reference.

. . . .   _____
(Type or print name of attorney)   (Signature of attorney)

I declare under penalty of perjury that, to the best of my knowledge, the foregoing is a true and correct listing of assets and obligations and that the amounts shown are correct; and that this declaration was executed on (date): . . . . at (place): . . . ., California.

. . . .   _____
(Type or print name)   (Signature)

ATTORNEY OR PARTY WITHOUT ATTORNEY (NAME AND ADDRESS):   TELEPHONE NO.:   FOR COURT USE ONLY

ATTORNEY FOR (NAME):

SUPERIOR COURT OF CALIFORNIA, COUNTY OF
STREET ADDRESS:
MAILING ADDRESS:
CITY AND ZIP CODE:
BRANCH NAME:

MARRIAGE OF
PETITIONER:

RESPONDENT:

INCOME AND EXPENSE DECLARATION
☐ PETITIONER ☐ RESPONDENT   CASE NUMBER:

GROSS MONTHLY INCOME	Petitioner	Respondent
1. Salary & wages (Include commissions, bonuses and overtime)	$	$
2. Pensions & retirement	$	$
3. Social Security	$	$
4. Disability and unemployment benefits	$	$
5. Public assistance (Welfare, AFDC payments, etc.)	$	$
6. Child/spousal support	$	$
7. Dividends and interest	$	$
8. Rents (gross receipts, less cash expenses; attach schedule)	$	$
9. Contributions to household expenses from other sources.	$	$
10. Income from all other sources (gross receipts, less cash expenses; attach schedule)	$	$
11. TOTAL GROSS MONTHLY INCOME	$	$

DEDUCTIONS FROM GROSS INCOME	Petitioner	Respondent
12. State income taxes	$	$
13. Federal income taxes	$	$
14. Social Security	$	$
15. State disability insurance . .	$	$
16. Medical and other insurance .	$	$
17. Union and other dues	$	$
18. Retirement and pension fund .	$	$
19. Savings plan	$	$
20. Other deductions (Specify) . .	$	$
21. TOTAL DEDUCTIONS	$	$

	Petitioner	Respondent
11. TOTAL GROSS MONTHLY INCOME (from line 11):	$	$
21. TOTAL DEDUCTIONS (From line 21):	$	$
22. NET MONTHLY INCOME (line 11 minus line 21)	$	$

23. Withholding information   a. Number of exemptions claimed: b. Marital status:

24. Certain property under the control of the parties

	Petitioner	Respondent
a. Cash & checking accounts	$	$ . . . .
b. Savings & credit union accounts	$	$ . . . .

	Petitioner	Respondent
c. Stocks, bonds, life insurance, other liquid assets.	$	$ . . . .
d. TOTAL (24a,b,c)	$	$ . . . .

The declaration under penalty of perjury must be signed in California or in a state that authorizes use of a declaration in place of an affidavit; otherwise an affidavit is required.

Form Adopted by Rule 1285.50
Judicial Council of California
Revised Effective January 1, 1980

**INCOME & EXPENSE DECLARATION
(FAMILY LAW)**

25. List the name, age, and relationship of all members of the household whose expenses are included below

MONTHLY EXPENSES	Petitioner	Respondent			Petitioner	Respondent
26. Residence payments				34. Child/spousal support (prior marriage)	$	$
a. Rent or mortgage	$	$				
b. Taxes & insurance	$	$		35. School	$	$
c. Maintenance	$	$		36. Entertainment	$	$
27. Food & household supplies	$	$		37. Incidentals	$	$
28. Utilities & telephone	$	$		38. Transportation & auto expenses (insurance, gas, oil, repair)	$	$
29. Laundry & cleaning	$	$		39. Installment payments (Insert total and itemize below at 42)	$	$
30. Clothing	$	$				
31. Medical & dental	$	$				
32. Insurance (life, health accident, etc.)	$	$		40. Other: (specify)	$	$
33. Child care	$	$		41. TOTAL MONTHLY EXPENSES	$	$

42. ITEMIZATION OF INSTALLMENT PAYMENTS OR OTHER DEBTS ☐ Continued on attachment 42.

CREDITOR'S NAME	FOR	MONTHLY PAYMENT	BALANCE
		$	$

43. ☐ ATTORNEY FEES HAVE BEEN REQUESTED.

a. I have paid my attorney for fees and costs the sum of $ . . . .   b. My arrangement for attorney fees and costs is:

. . . .   _____
(Print or type name of Attorney)   (Signature of Attorney)

I declare under penalty of perjury that the foregoing, including any attachment, is true and correct and that this declaration is executed at (place): . . . . , California, on (date): . . . .

. . . .   _____
(Print or type name of Declarant)   (Signature of Declarant)

ATTORNEY OR PARTY WITHOUT ATTORNEY (NAME AND ADDRESS):	TELEPHONE NO.:	FOR COURT USE ONLY
ATTORNEY FOR (NAME):		

SUPERIOR COURT OF CALIFORNIA, COUNTY OF
STREET ADDRESS:
MAILING ADDRESS:
CITY AND ZIP CODE:
BRANCH NAME:

MARRIAGE OF

PETITIONER:

RESPONDENT:

INTERLOCUTORY JUDGMENT OF DISSOLUTION OF MARRIAGE	CASE NUMBER:

1. This proceeding came on for ☐ default or uncontested ☐ contested hearing as follows

   a. Date: ☐ Dept.: ☐ Div.: ☐ Room:

   b. Judge (name): ☐ Temporary judge

   c. ☐ Petitioner present in court ☐ Attorney present in court (name):

   d. ☐ Respondent present in court ☐ Attorney present in court (name):

   e. ☐ Claimant present in court ☐ Attorney present in court (name):

2. The court acquired jurisdiction of the respondent on (date):
   a. ☐ Respondent was served with process.
   b. ☐ Respondent appeared.

3. THE COURT ORDERS
   a. An interlocutory judgment be entered and the parties are entitled to have their marriage dissolved.

   b. After six months from the date the court acquired jurisdiction of the respondent a final judgment of dissolution may be entered upon proper application of either party or on the court's own motion, unless a dismissal signed by both parties is filed. The final judgment shall include such other and further relief as may be necessary to a complete disposition of this proceeding, but entry of the final judgment shall not deprive this court of its jurisdiction over any matter expressly reserved to it in this or the final judgment until a final disposition is made of each such matter.

   c. Jurisdiction is reserved to make such other and further orders as may be necessary to carry out the provisions of this judgment.

4. ☐ THE COURT FURTHER ORDERS
   a. ☐ Wife's former name be restored (specify):
   b. ☐ Other:

Dated: . . . .

_____
Judge of the Superior Court

5. Total number of pages attached: ☐ Signature follows last attachment

THIS INTERLOCUTORY JUDGMENT DOES NOT CONSTITUTE A FINAL DISSOLUTION OF MARRIAGE AND THE PARTIES ARE STILL MARRIED. ONE OF THE PARTIES MUST SUBMIT A REQUEST FOR FINAL JUDGMENT ON THE FORM PRESCRIBED BY RULE 1288. NEITHER PARTY MAY REMARRY UNTIL A FINAL JUDGMENT OF DISSOLUTION IS ENTERED.

ALTHOUGH AN OBLIGATION BASED ON A CONTRACT IS ASSIGNED TO ONE PARTY AS PART OF THE DIVISION OF THE COMMUNITY, IF THE PARTY TO WHOM THE OBLIGATION WAS ASSIGNED DEFAULTS ON THE CONTRACT, THE CREDITOR MAY HAVE A CAUSE OF ACTION AGAINST THE OTHER PARTY.

No attachment permitted on less than a full page. Cal Rule of Ct 201(b)

Form Adopted by Rule 1287
Judicial Council of California
Revised Effective January 1, 1981

**INTERLOCUTORY JUDGMENT OF
DISSOLUTION OF MARRIAGE
(FAMILY LAW)**

CC 4512, 4514

ATTORNEY OR PARTY WITHOUT ATTORNEY (NAME AND ADDRESS):	TELEPHONE NO.:	FOR COURT USE ONLY
ATTORNEY FOR (NAME):		

SUPERIOR COURT OF CALIFORNIA, COUNTY OF
STREET ADDRESS:
MAILING ADDRESS:
CITY AND ZIP CODE:
BRANCH NAME:

MARRIAGE OF
PETITIONER:

RESPONDENT:

NOTICE OF ENTRY OF JUDGMENT	CASE NUMBER:

You are notified that the following judgment was entered on (date):

1. ☐ Interlocutory Judgment of Dissolution of Marriage

> THE INTERLOCUTORY JUDGMENT TO WHICH THIS NOTICE REFERS **DOES NOT CONSTITUTE A FINAL DISSOLUTION OF MARRIAGE AND THE PARTIES ARE STILL MARRIED. ONE OF THE PARTIES MUST SUBMIT A REQUEST FOR A FINAL JUDGMENT ON THE FORM PRESCRIBED BY RULE 1288.** NEITHER PARTY MAY REMARRY UNTIL A FINAL JUDGMENT OF DISSOLUTION **IS ENTERED.**

2. ☐ Final Judgment of Dissolution of Marriage
3. ☐ Final Judgment of Legal Separation
4. ☐ Final Judgment of Nullity

Dated: . . . . Clerk, By _____ , **Deputy**

CLERK'S CERTIFICATE OF MAILING

I certify that I am not a party to this cause and that a copy of the foregoing was mailed **first class, postage prepaid,** in a sealed envelope addressed as shown below, and that the mailing of the foregoing **and execution of this certificate** occurred at (place): . . . . **, California,**

on (date): . . . . Clerk, By _____ , **Deputy**

Form Adopted by Rule 1290
Judicial Council of California
Revised Effective January 1, 1980

NOTICE OF ENTRY OF JUDGMENT
(FAMILY LAW)

ATTORNEY OR PARTY WITHOUT ATTORNEY (NAME AND ADDRESS)	TELEPHONE NO.:	FOR COURT USE ONLY
ATTORNEY FOR (NAME):		

SUPERIOR COURT OF CALIFORNIA, COUNTY OF
STREET ADDRESS:
MAILING ADDRESS:
CITY AND ZIP CODE:
BRANCH NAME:

MARRIAGE OF

PETITIONER:

RESPONDENT:

REQUEST AND DECLARATION FOR FINAL JUDGMENT OF DISSOLUTION OF MARRIAGE	CASE NUMBER:

1. The court acquired jurisdiction of the respondent on (date):

2. An Interlocutory Judgment of Dissolution of Marriage was entered on (date):

3. Since entry of the Interlocutory Judgment the parties have not become reconciled and have not agreed to dismiss this proceeding. No motion or other proceeding to set aside or annul, and no appeal from that part of the interlocutory judgment granting dissolution of the marriage, is pending and undetermined, and that part of the judgment has become final.

4. I request that final judgment of dissolution of marriage be entered.
   a. ☐ Endorsed copies of a Joint Petition for Summary Dissolution and a Notice of Revocation are attached and I request entry of final judgment pursuant to Civil Code section 4514(b).
   b. ☐ I request judgment be entered effective (nunc pro tunc)
      (1) As of (date):
      (2) For the following reason:

5. ☐ Other request (specify):

6. I declare under penalty of perjury that the foregoing is true and correct and that this declaration is executed on (date): . . . . at (place): . . . . , California.

. . . .   _____
(Type or print name)   (Signature of declarant)

. . . .   _____
(Type or print name)   (Signature of attorney for declarant)

The declaration under penalty of perjury must be signed in California, or in a state that authorizes use of a declaration in place of an affidavit; otherwise an affidavit is required.

Form Adopted by Rule 1288
Judicial Council of California
Revised Effective January 1, 1980

REQUEST AND DECLARATION FOR FINAL JUDGMENT OF DISSOLUTION OF MARRIAGE (FAMILY LAW)

CC 4514, 4515

ATTORNEY OR PARTY WITHOUT ATTORNEY (NAME AND ADDRESS):	TELEPHONE:	FOR COURT USE ONLY
ATTORNEY FOR (Name):		

SUPERIOR COURT OF CALIFORNIA, COUNTY OF
STREET ADDRESS:
MAILING ADDRESS:
CITY AND ZIP CODE:
BRANCH NAME:

MARRIAGE OF
PETITIONER:

RESPONDENT:

FINAL JUDGMENT OF ☐ DISSOLUTION OF MARRIAGE ☐ LEGAL SEPARATION ☐ NULLITY ☐ DISSOLUTION OF MARRIAGE—STATUS ONLY	CASE NUMBER:

1. The court acquired jurisdiction of the respondent on (date):

2. THE COURT ORDERS
   a. ☐ A final judgment of dissolution be entered, and the parties are restored to the status of unmarried persons.
   b. ☐ A judgment of legal separation be entered.
   c. ☐ A judgment of nullity be entered on the ground of (specify):

   and the parties are declared to be unmarried persons.

3. ☐ THE COURT FURTHER ORDERS
   a. ☐ This judgment be entered nunc pro tunc as of (date):
   b. ☐ Wife's former name be restored (specify):
   c. ☐ Other (specify):

Dated: . . . . _____
                                        Judge of the Superior Court

                               ☐ Signature follows last attachment.

4. Total number of pages attached:

NOTICE

1. PLEASE REVIEW YOUR WILL. UNLESS A PROVISION IS MADE IN THE PROPERTY SETTLEMENT AGREEMENT, THIS COURT PROCEEDING DOES NOT AFFECT YOUR WILL AND THE ABILITY OF YOUR FORMER SPOUSE TO TAKE UNDER IT.

2. ALTHOUGH AN OBLIGATION BASED ON A CONTRACT IS ASSIGNED TO ONE PARTY AS PART OF THE DIVISION OF THE COMMUNITY, IF THE PARTY TO WHOM THE OBLIGATION WAS ASSIGNED DEFAULTS ON THE CONTRACT, THE CREDITOR MAY HAVE A CAUSE OF ACTION AGAINST THE OTHER PARTY.

3. IF YOU FAIL TO PAY ANY COURT ORDERED CHILD SUPPORT, AN ASSIGNMENT OF YOUR WAGES WILL BE OBTAINED WITHOUT FURTHER NOTICE TO YOU.

No attachment permitted on less than a full page. Cal. Rules of Court, rule 201(b).

Form Adopted by Rule 1289
Judicial Council of California
Revised Effective January 1, 1982

**FINAL JUDGMENT
(FAMILY LAW)**

CC 4514, 4515

SUPERIOR COURT OF CALIFORNIA, COUNTY OF

STREET ADDRESS:

MAILING ADDRESS:

CITY AND ZIP CODE:

BRANCH NAME:

MARRIAGE OF

PETITIONER:

RESPONDENT:

NOTICE OF ENTRY OF JUDGMENT

CASE NUMBER:

You are notified that the following judgment was entered on (date):

1. ☐ Interlocutory Judgment of Dissolution of Marriage

THE INTERLOCUTORY JUDGMENT TO WHICH THIS NOTICE REFERS DOES NOT CONSTITUTE A FINAL DISSOLUTION OF MARRIAGE AND THE PARTIES ARE STILL MARRIED. ONE OF THE PARTIES MUST SUBMIT A REQUEST FOR A FINAL JUDGMENT ON THE FORM PRESCRIBED BY RULE 1288. NEITHER PARTY MAY REMARRY UNTIL A FINAL JUDGMENT OF DISSOLUTION IS ENTERED.

2. ☐ Final Judgment of Dissolution of Marriage
3. ☐ Final Judgment of Legal Separation
4. ☐ Final Judgment of Nullity

Dated: . . . . Clerk, By _____ , Deputy

CLERK'S CERTIFICATE OF MAILING

I certify that I am not a party to this cause and that a copy of the foregoing was mailed first class, postage prepaid, in a sealed envelope addressed as shown below, and that the mailing of the foregoing and execution of this certificate occurred at (place): . . . . , California,

on (date): . . . . Clerk, By _____ , Deputy

**NOTICE OF ENTRY OF JUDGMENT
(FAMILY LAW)**

OTHER BOOKS AVAILABLE FROM NOLO PRESS

Nolo Press was born about ten years ago with this book, "How to Do Your Own Divorce in California." Since then, we have published twelve more books to help you with other legal procedures. We offer for sale another six books published by independent authors not affiliated with Nolo Press, because they are similar to our own philosophy. Following is a brief description of each of these books, and an order coupon to make it easy for you to order any (or all!) of them.

Titles planned for next year will deal with bankruptcy, gay rights, search for adopteds and business partnerships. If there are other areas that you would like to suggest, we would be glad to hear from you.

ORDER BLANK

Your Name _____

Street Address _____

Town, State, Zip Code _____

Please send me the following books, as described on the next two pages:

Quantity	Title	Price

Please enclose check or money order and send to:

NOLO PRESS
P.O. Box 544
Occidental, CA 95465
OR
950 Parker St.
Berkeley, CA 94710

Subtotal _____

6% sales tax _____

75 cents each postage _____

TOTAL _____

OTHER BOOKS PUBLISHED
BY NOLO PRESS

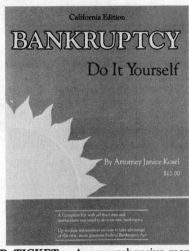